CISTERCIAN STUDIES SERIES: NUMBER ONE HUNDRED EIGHTY-EIGHT

FROM ADVENT TO PENTECOST

D1089669

Other books in the Carthusian Novice Conferences series

The Call of Silent Love
The Way of Silent Love
Interior Prayer
The Freedom of Obedience
Poor, Therefore Rich

Other Carthusian books

The Wound of Love: A Carthusian Miscellany
They Speak by Silences
Where Silence is Praise
The Spirit of Place
The Meditations of Guigo, Prior of The Charterhouse
The Ladder of Monks and Twelve Meditations

Compact Disc

In the Silence of the Word: A Carthusian Plainchant Meditation

CISTERCIAN STUDIES SERIES: NUMBER ONE HUNDRED EIGHTY-EIGHT

FROM ADVENT TO PENTECOST

Carthusian Novice Conferences

by a Carthusian

Translated by
Carmel Brett

CISTERCIAN PUBLICATIONS

Kalamazoo, Michigan — Spencer, Massachusetts

First published in 1999 by
Darton, Longman and Todd Ltd
1 Spencer Court
140–142 Wandsworth High Street
London SW18 4JJ
and by
Cistercian Publications
WMU Station
Kalamazoo, Michigan 49008

ISBN 0 87907 788 3

A catalogue record for this book is available from the British Library

Acknowledgements
Grateful acknowledgement is extended to Carmel Brett for the
translation from the French, done with a great love of Carthusian
liturgy; Jennifer Wild for very perceptive adaptation and editing work;
and a young Carthusian monk for meticulous correcting and a vigilant
theological eye. For much labour, many thanks.

Phototypeset by Intype London Ltd
Printed and bound in Great Britain by
Redwood Books, Trowbridge, Wiltshire

Contents

Introduction

From the beginning of the Carthusian Order in the eleventh century, we have used a liturgy that is proper to us, but borrowed from different traditions, mostly of Roman origin. From the Council of Trent on, we kept our own liturgy while integrating some new feasts, keeping in touch with the life and devotions of the Church. In the wake of Vatican II, this Carthusian liturgy has been renewed, while retaining its character of a proper rite with its own calendar, Office, Missal and Lectionary.

To make it simple, most of the Sunday readings of the Lectionary (for Mass) are the same as those of the old Roman lectionary. The choice of biblical readings has been enlarged for weekdays, feasts and the Common of the Saints in order to include texts in harmony with a contemplative vocation.

Walking along beaches of the sea and beds of rivers, we find pebbles. This is not their initial shape. They were sharp, rugged stones at first. But the current of the river or the movement of the sea have shaped them into what they are. Year after year, season after season, tides and waves remove one grain here, another there. The process is slow but the work is better done that way than by any human tool, hammer or chisel.

The Liturgy is a sea. We are plunged into it and transformed by it. Year after year the liturgical seasons come back, like the tides over stones: Advent, Christmastide, Lent, Eastertide, Ordinary Time. Always the same cycle, but shaping us, slowly but surely, into *living stones* (1 Peter 2:5).

As living stones, we are as different as pebbles are from one another. Both the nature of the stone and the place it is in have made it evolve this or that way. A stone thrown into a river will not be the same as one thrown into the sea near a beach. A

Charterhouse is a small community of hermits. Its tides are simple and sober. Those reading this book may find at the same time the wide sea – the Liturgy of the whole Church, and what is specific to a small river – the haven of the Charterhouse.

ADVENT

1

Hope

Advent is a time of hope totally intent upon the joy to come. It invites us to look towards the goal proposed to us by the Word of God through the grand vision of the Prophets, especially that of Isaiah.

Several among you are beginning your monastic life at this moment. Let us try to allow ourselves to be taught very simply by the Word of God about the magnificent dimensions of his promises, in order to follow Christ with courage and confidence. At the beginning of every work, look to the end. In the hierarchy of the theological virtues, hope is 'an insignificant little girl' beside her two big sisters, faith and charity. And nevertheless, it is she 'who moves the others' (Péguy). If we did not expect a great good, if we did not believe it possible, we would not be capable of any effort.

Also, the confidence and joy of a hope that is rightly understood are very important. They give a new tonality to the spiritual life, conferring upon it that lightness and beauty, that radiant something which allows one to bear the exigencies of religious life and its renunciations in a joyful way. It is not enough to do good, said St Francis de Sales, one must do it cheerfully. God loves him who gives with joy. That joy is a refinement of love. From the first day, therefore, let us stamp the mark of confidence and audacity on our spiritual life.

THE OBJECT OF OUR HOPE

'Hope is a supernatural virtue whereby we confidently expect from God his grace in this world and eternal glory in the next' (Old Cathechism).

What is this eternal glory? It is God giving himself to us with all that he is and all that he has. God gives himself as God, or he does not give himself at all. God is simple. There is no division in him. Each one receives this infinite gift according to the capacity of his love.

This is our hope. Let us become aware of its enormous audacity. Us, minute creatures of a moment, us, moulded with the clay of the earth, bearers of the fragile breath of our spirit, powerless, sinners. God, greater than the whole of creation, all-powerful, immense, infinite, holy, pure spirit.

If you look closely, you will see that I have said nothing about what God is in himself. That is entirely hidden from me. God, for me, is an impenetrable mystery. I can only name him in comparison with creatures, ascribing to him the perfection of whatever exists in an imperfect state in creatures. I know that God is more unlike than like all I can attribute to him – even all that Sacred Scripture says of him, because it speaks the language of humankind.

So what do I do? Be silent? No. I can speak of Christ, he who is God coming close to us, becoming like us. In him the perfect union between God and humankind has been realised. Our hope is to participate in that union, to become sons in the Son – 'Christ in you, the hope of glory' (Colossians 1:27).

Christ, our hope
The dimensions of our hope are the dimensions of Christ. Our inheritance is so great that only the Father can reveal it to us. Let us open our heart to that light.

> I pray that the God of our Lord Jesus Christ, the Father of glory, may give you a spirit of wisdom and revelation as you come to know him, so that, with the eyes of your heart enlightened, you may know what is the hope to which he has called you, what are the riches of his glorious inheritance among the saints, and what is the immeasurable greatness of his power for us who believe, according to the working of his great power... in Christ... (Ephesians 1:17–19)

Christ embraces the whole of creation: 'in him all things in heaven and on earth were created'. 'All things have been created through him and for him' (Colossians 1:16). For God's plan is to 'gather up all things in [Christ], things in heaven and things on earth' (Ephesians 1:10).

I do not hope for health, success, happiness in human terms, not even for human love. I do not even hope for a supernatural happiness for myself alone. I hope, God enables me to hope for only one thing: Christ. For myself, of course, but not only for myself. More, for those I love. For all humankind, for all creation, I hope, with confidence in the Word of God, for that fullness of life and love which is the full stature of Christ, God all in all.

The dimensions of solitude

If we choose to live in a little cell, to restrict our contacts with our brothers and with the world, it is not in order to live a narrow existence, locked into our little ego. On the contrary, it is in order to open our heart to the dimensions of Christ's heart, in order to embrace the whole of humanity in our love, in order to carry the whole universe in our prayer and our praise.

In a similar way, an astronomer closes one of his eyes and fixes the other on the narrow opening of a large telescope, not to avoid seeing what immediately surrounds him, but in order to project his gaze into the immensity of stellar space. If we recollect ourselves in our heart by plunging within ourselves, it is not to exclude others, but to reach that ground of our being which rightly goes beyond our individual self and opens upon the divine space. There we rediscover ourselves and we rediscover our brothers in that eternal love which is the ultimate truth of us all – ' . . . that they may all be one. As you, Father, are in me and I am in you, may they also be in us . . . so that the love with which you have loved me may be in them, and I in them' (John 17:21, 26b).

These are the dimensions of our solitude! The smaller the cell, the bigger our vision should be. One must have a broad and open spirit in order to live in solitude. Let us not allow anything to restrict it to what is less than Christ. Let us mercilessly shatter the partitions of our egoism, the preoccupation (even pious) we have with ourselves, the anxieties about our perfection, about the Order, etc. Let us seek the Kingdom of God. It is in us. Let us live there constantly. Let us be lost to all that is not Christ, and to ourselves as well. Let us always reply: 'Why were you searching for me? Did you not know that I must be in my Father's house?' (Luke 2:49). Do you realise? It is to his most holy mother and to St Joseph that Christ addresses those words.

Note that the Advent liturgy, from the first week, puts before us the mystery of Christ in its broadest eschatological dimensions. Do likewise, you who, this Advent, begin the liturgy of your life of prayer in the Charterhouse.

THE NECESSARY MEANS

The very greatness of that vision could itself discourage us. We know ourselves to be weak, poor, sinners. If we have to depend on our own strength, we shall not go far, that is certain.

> We have become like one who is unclean,
>   and all our righteous deeds are like a filthy cloth.
> We all fade like a leaf,
>   and our iniquities, like the wind, take us away.
>
> (Isaiah 64:6–7)

Let us not listen to the word of the prophets as if it were a matter of a message addressed to Israel at a moment in the past, which would have only an historical interest for us. Certainly, the promise it contains was realised partly in contemporary events. But that does not in any way exhaust the vision of the prophet who, beyond that realisation and still others, has in view, above all, the final eschatological accomplishment, when the Kingdom of God will establish itself over every creature. This final accomplishment has begun in Christ; it is realised in his individual, glorified humanity, but not yet in his body which is the Church. That is the reason why the Liturgy makes us read the great promises of the prophets, above all Isaiah, during this time of expectancy. The

Christian life on earth is a time of expectancy. The life of the monk is especially so.

The promises of God
But if the Word of God takes away from us all self-complacency, it does not leave us without hope. On the contrary, it never ceases to cry:

> 'Be strong, do not fear!
> Here is your God . . .
> He will come and save you.
>
> (Isaiah 35:4)

Let us remember that promise in the long combat of the spiritual life, of prayer. Above all let us not despair when we remain dry, alone, distant, poor. The Lord will come. The fountains of our tears will flow. The water of prayer will spring forth in love. The Lord is faithful.

If we can do nothing by ourselves, the Lord can do all things. Blessed poverty, which forces God himself to come to our aid!

> I will open rivers on the bare heights,
>   and fountains in the midst of the valleys;
> I will make the wilderness a pool of water,
>   and the dry land springs of water.
>
> (Isaiah 41:18)

The Word made flesh
The Lord has come. The Word was made flesh, one day, 2,000 years ago, in Bethlehem. He was born in the heart of each one of us on the day of our Baptism. We enter ever more deeply into that birth every Christmas. The total Christ will be fully accomplished on the day of the Parousia.

The power of the Spirit
We have received the first-fruits of the Holy Spirit. The Spirit raised up Christ. He will raise us up in turn. The entire creation has been sown by the Word with a hidden seed of life.

It is pregnant with a new life to which it aspires in an obscure way.

> We know that the whole creation has been groaning in labour pains until now; and not only creation, but we ourselves, who have the first fruits of the Spirit, groan inwardly while we wait for adoption, the redemption of our bodies. (Romans 8:22–23)

The Christian life is entirely set between the two poles of a consummation that is at once already present and yet still hidden and to come. Only the Spirit of Christ in us can express our desire, because only he truly knows what we desire. 'We do not know how to pray as we ought, but that very Spirit intercedes with sighs too deep for words . . .' (Romans 8:26).

Hope is not only a desire, but a desire which believes that it will reach its goal, which is certain of that. The work which he began in Christ, God will bring to good completion.

> Those whom he predestined he also called; and those whom he called he also justified; and those whom he justified he also glorified. (Romans 8:30)

> For if, while we were enemies, we were reconciled to God through the death of his Son, much more surely, having been reconciled, will we be saved by his life. (Romans 5:10)

Always, by the Spirit.

The love of God, in Christ
Our certainty is founded on the love of God manifested and given definitively to us, to all humankind, in Christ. Nothing can shake it.

> For I am convinced that neither death nor life, nor angels, nor rulers, nor things present, nor things to come, nor powers, nor height, nor depth, nor anything else in all creation, will be able to separate us from the love of God in Christ Jesus our Lord. (Romans 8:38–39)

Note it well: our hope does not rest at all on our virtue, nor on our merits, nor on others. We hope for that which can only be an absolutely gratuitous gift of God; the intimate union of love (Song of Solomon 8:7). Otherwise, we are sinners. Our hope rests entirely on God, on Christ. It is born of faith and charity.

Why do you not perform miracles?
'What charisms are there among you? Why do you not perform miracles?' a young charismatic asked me one day. Is it that we lack that living faith which passes without intermediary from the promises of the Gospel to their fulfilment in life? Alas! we partly do lack it, I believe. However, our life is a life hidden in Christ. The true miracle which we hope for is the transformation of our poverty into the love of Christ – a way superior to the others, said St Paul (1 Corinthians 12:31). Let us hope for that with all our strength: love in us and among us. For the object of hope is God. And God is love. If there is a charism among us, if it is in the interest of the Church, may it be the charism of prayer, humble and pure of heart. Mary, the mother of Jesus and Mary of Bethany, among others, did not perform miracles.

The riches of the poor
Because we can do nothing of ourselves, we can do all things in him who gives us strength (Philippians 4:13). The more poor and empty of ourselves we are, the more pure and powerful is our hope. When, in practice, we rely on our talents, our human potential etc., we quickly reach our limits and, in the supernatural realm, we do nothing important. When, on the contrary, we stake everything on God, nothing is impossible to us, because 'for God all things are possible' (Matthew 19:26). Carve that word of Christ in your heart.

The road which is opening before you seems hard and long to you. So it is. You are conscious of your weaknesses, of your inconstancy, of the little light you possess. That is the truth. And yet it is indeed you whom Christ has called to follow him at close quarters. Were the apostles any better? Such is the signature of God whose 'power is at its best in weakness'. It is the sign of the Cross. Repeat this word of St Paul: 'Whenever I am weak, then I am strong' (2 Corinthians 12:10) – not with my own strength but with the omnipotence of Christ.

Do not ever yield to despair. Be poor, be sinners, be weak, but always hope. Never can your trust in the Lord be too great. No obstacle is insurmountable for his strength.

> I know the one in whom I have put my trust. (2 Timothy 1:12)

> The Lord is my strength and my shield;
>   in him my heart trusts;
> so I am helped.
>
> (Psalm 28:7)

> Wait for the Lord;
>   be strong, and let your heart take courage;
>   wait for the Lord!
>
> (Psalm 27:14)

The dynamism of Hope

Hope is powerful. To rely on God alone does not mean to yield to inertia. The hope of faith makes the strength of the Spirit enter into us, and this power unfolds with an activity the more effective the more it is God's action rather than ours.

> Work out your own salvation with fear and trembling; for it is God who is at work in you, enabling you both to will and to work for his good pleasure. (Philippians 2:12–13)

Presumption is also a disorder of hope. We hope for everything through faith in Christ. It is grace which does its works in us. And nevertheless, we are invited to put everything to work as if everything depended on us. A contradiction? A mystery, rather. The mystery of grace and of our freedom.

Let us pray, let us humble ourselves, let us open our hearts to the power of God, let us always have recourse to the Lord in all that we do, let us allow him to act in us, let us abandon everything into his hands. Then let us follow the impulse of grace, let us do all we can at our humble level, with courage, intelligence and energy.

Hope frees all our vital energies, even when it is a matter of 'worldly' works. When that light does not shine, the horizon is walled up, nothing is worthwhile, all is despair, suicide or a life which refuses to emerge from a sort of material prolongation, an existence without relief, like the path of a quenched star.

We monks should be a spark of hope in the heart of a world where the darkness of despair triumphs in too many people. Let us reflect on to them the light which Christ has shone in our hearts (2 Corinthians 4:6), by our joy and our confidence. Let us hope for those who have no hope. All of us, in Christ, are one. If we ourselves feel we are in the dark, so much the better – hope is not a film of the future; the mystery remains.

Rising out of the obscure mass of humanity, our hope and our prayer can raise up all humankind towards the light, towards Christ.

May the God of hope fill you with all joy and peace in believing, so that you may abound in hope by the power of the Holy Spirit. (Romans 15:13)

2

He Who Comes

'Hope springs eternal in the human breast,' said the poet Alexander Pope. We live always in expectation of something. A tomorrow that will go better. Look at the eyes of a child; they are full of hope. Everything is possible. With time, what one calls the 'principle of reality' makes the hard limits of the possible felt, the dream shrinks and runs the risk of dissolving into a disillusioned surrender. The heart gets old, hardens. The extreme paradox are those modern men described, for example in the plays of Ionesco and Samuel Becket: despoiled of all hope, they live, so to speak, in pure expectancy. An absurd expectancy without an object, nonetheless an expectancy. Of what? Of whom? No one knows and yet, after each disappointment an expectancy is reborn. Tomorrow, perhaps . . . someone will come . . . something will happen . . . It is already a victory over the death of deep forces buried in the heart before the death of despair.

Their intuition is correct. The real world borders on the little world of appearances and of the insignificant. One is right to wait, to dream. Paradoxically, we do not dream enough, do not aim high enough. There are thrilling dimensions of the real, spaces wider than even those a child dreams of, where the heart can open out into infinity, an infinity which exists and whose dimensions are revealed to us by faith.

The liturgical season of Advent makes us enter into that world. The words Advent, Christmas, Epiphany had, in profane usage, nearly the same meaning at the epoch (sixth century) when the season of Advent was added, in the West, to the two Solemnities of the Birth of the Lord and his Manifestation (in Greek, epiphany). The three words were used to designate the accession of a sovereign or his triumphal entry into a city. The

Liturgy applies them to Christ, having regard above all to his second coming in glory. The first coming is the time of his passage through his incarnation, death and resurrection to the glory of the Father.

It is significant that the date of the feast of Christmas, 25 December (the winter solstice), was originally in the West the date of a pagan festival consecrated to the sun, the same festival being celebrated on 6 January in the East. We do not know the historical date of the birth of Christ. Obviously the Church chose these dates in order to oppose to the pagan cult – one of the last which still resisted at the time – him who is the true Light. That is one of the reasons for the insistence on the theme of the light – which is in any case biblical.

In our liturgical books, the liturgical year begins with Advent: But Advent itself begins with a week which evokes the glorious return of the Lord, the culmination of the whole history of salvation. We begin therefore at the end! But this is very good, because in moral matters one must first aim at the goal, and only then choose the means to accomplish it. In the matter of the Christian life, we must know where we are going in order to know how to set about getting there. And it is clear that the whole history of the universe is moving towards the second coming of the Lord, where the final judgement of all people will come to pass, where our present world will come to an end, and the new earth and the new heavens to replace it will unfold; in short, the full actualisation of the Kingdom of God, where God will be all in all.

There is the object of our faith in all its grandeur. Turned towards him, Christians can only desire and call for that coming of Christ, with all our prayer. Let us think of the empty throne of the Pantocrator in the ancient mosaics of certain churches in Rome and Ravenna.

Advent is therefore not only a preparation so that we can better commemorate the birth of Christ in Bethlehem. It is that, certainly, but it is more the expression of the joyful hope of the return of the Lord. And as the Kingdom of God is already in us by the presence of Christ in our hearts, by the grace of the Spirit we go forward towards the encounter with the Lord, in so far as the Word of God is born in our hearts, or, more exactly, in so far as we enter into the divine life, in the Word, becoming sons in the Son.

STRUCTURE OF THE ADVENT SEASON

Let us recall that the liturgical year comes to a close with the feast of Christ the King, with an orientation above all eschatological. It is the King of the Last Judgement, of the Kingdom of God in heaven, who is celebrated in all his majesty.

The first week of Advent continues along on the same theme, but this is presented above all as an object of hope in the expectation of Christ's return.

The second and third weeks are centred on John the Baptist: in his person the prophetic expectation of the Old Testament becomes urgent and immediate. His finger points to the Messiah, present at last. He is there in the midst of us, and our hearts must be purified and made ready for him.

From 17 December onwards, the Liturgy prepares us directly to commemorate the birth of Christ with a more living faith. For seven days, prophecies and fulfilments respond to each other in the readings of the Mass provided for each day. Mary is at the centre of it, Mary, the expectant mother who carries the child towards the birth on which everything converges.

All of these themes are summed up in the great 'O' antiphons of the Magnificat, from 17 to 24 December. There at one and the same time are incomparably expressed the messianic expectation of the Old Testament, the greatness of the incarnate Word and the 'Veni' ('Come!'), bearer of all the present hope of the Church and of humanity. The intercessory prayers of the Office, inspired by these antiphons, give a note of expectancy and desire to our prayer.

The Alpha and the Omega

The beautiful melody of the First Vespers hymn for the First Sunday of Advent immediately puts us into the atmosphere characteristic of this season. Let us notice, what is more, the extent of the vision, embodying the whole work of salvation, the work of the divine compassion for the sufferings of fallen humanity, right up to the final judgement. The Scripture reading sounds the specific note of the week:

> Look! He is coming with the clouds;
>   every eye will see him . . .
> So it is to be. Amen.
> 'I am the Alpha and the Omega,' says the Lord God, who is and who was and who is to come, the Almighty. (Revelation 1:7–8)

The glorious Christ of the Apocalypse, established in the eternity of God, is Lord over time. He is the One who is, who was and who is to come. His second coming is evoked in the words of the prophetic vision of Daniel, of the Son of man coming among the clouds to receive from God 'dominion and glory and kingship' (Daniel 7:14).

Matins
The first response of Matins summarises the grand vision of Daniel. The seven responses that follow contain messianic prophecies of other prophets, above all Isaiah. The first three responses of the third nocturn already evoke the fulfilment in the annunciation to Mary; the twelfth response permits St Paul to express the peculiarly Christian hope:

> It is from [heaven] that we are expecting a Saviour, the Lord Jesus Christ. He will transform the body of our humiliation so that it may be conformed to the body of his glory . . . (Philippians 3:20–21)

Nearly all the Advent themes are thus present in the office of Matins, because the Liturgy does not establish watertight compartments. It offers a presence of the whole mystery in all its facets, but with one or other aspect more prominent in any given place.

The biblical readings of Matins for Advent are drawn from Isaiah, who knew how to sing, in a lyrical poetry unequalled in the Bible, the hope of a universal salvation. The Lord himself is going to intervene in human history to inaugurate his reign.

The two advents of the Messiah in the prophets: Isaiah
Isaiah, like all the prophets, telescopes the planes of time. He describes in vision, as contemporary, events which in reality are separated by great intervals. It is a little like seeing, from a long way off, two mountains that are actually situated at a great distance from each other – they appear to be both on the same plane; but on nearing the foothills of the first, one can see that the second is still far ahead.

Likewise, one can distinguish in the prophets two aspects, apparently contradictory, of the coming of the Messiah, the awaited Saviour; this contradiction disappears if one considers them as relating to two successive comings, as we do quite naturally on reading them in the light of Christ.

Isaiah, for example, describes the Messiah as a suffering Servant, mocked and humiliated, who by his sufferings and his death justifies the multitude (Isaiah 52 and 53). On the other hand, the same book of Isaiah describes the Messiah coming in glory, the very glory of God. Jesus himself invokes that prophecy when the disciples of John the Baptist ask him if he is indeed 'the One who is to come' (Matthew 11:2–6: we read these texts on the second Sunday of Advent).

> The wilderness and the dry land shall be glad . . .
> They shall see the glory of the Lord,
>   the majesty of our God . . .
> 'Be strong, do not fear!
> Here is your God . . .
> He will come and save you.'
>
> (Isaiah 35:1, 2, 4)

Daniel
Daniel also foresees two events, one in history, the other at the end of time.

In a first vision we find the strange image of the stone which grows and spreads.

> [The] statue was huge, its brilliance extraordinary; it was standing before you, and its appearance was frightening. The head of that statue was of fine gold, its chest and arms

of silver, its middle and thighs of bronze, its legs of iron, its feet partly of iron and partly of clay. As you looked on, a stone was cut out, not by human hands, and it struck the statue on its feet of iron and clay and broke them in pieces. Then the iron, the clay, the bronze, the silver, and the gold, were all broken in pieces and . . . the wind carried them away, so that not a trace of them could be found. But the stone that struck the statue became a great mountain and filled the whole earth. (Daniel 2:31–36)

Interpreting the dream, Daniel sees in the four elements that make up the statue the succession of four great kingdoms. The last kingdom, the one symbolised by the feet, is a divided kingdom possessing in itself strength and weakness. The stone is likewise a kingdom, but unlike the others this kingdom is set up by the God of heaven and this is a kingdom 'that shall never be destroyed' (Daniel 2:44).

That simple stone which breaks away untouched by human hand but which makes the huge statue fly into pieces indicates the historical process set in motion by the first coming of the Messiah.

The Fathers liked to see in the stone the image of Christ born of the Virgin without the intervention of a father according to the flesh. He is in fact the living stone upon whom rests the entire edifice.

A second vision of Daniel was applied by Jesus himself to his return in glory (Matthew 24:30). He quoted it before Caiphas, provoking thus his sentence to death as a blasphemer.

As I watched in the night visions,
I saw one like a human being
    coming with the clouds of heaven.
And he came to the Ancient One
    and was presented before him.
To him was given dominion
    and glory and kingship,
that all peoples, nations, and languages
    should serve him.

> His dominion is an everlasting dominion
>> that shall not pass away,
> and his kingship is one
>> that shall never be destroyed.

(Daniel 7:13–14)

Zechariah

This prophet also describes the Messiah as at one time humble and suffering, at another time all-powerful and glorious. 'Lo, your king comes to you; triumphant and glorious is he ... humble and riding on a donkey, on a colt, the foal of a donkey' (Zechariah 9:9). The evangelist John (12:16) tells us that the disciples of Jesus after his Resurrection 'remembered that these things had been written of him and had been done to him' on Palm Sunday when he made his entry into Jerusalem. The prophet Zechariah writes in chapter 12:10–12:

> When they look on the one whom they have pierced, they shall mourn for him as one mourns for an only child, and weep bitterly over him as one weeps over a firstborn ... The land shall mourn.

By contrast, in chapter 14 Zechariah describes for us the glorious and all-powerful Christ:

> On that day his feet shall stand on the Mount of Olives, which lies before Jerusalem on the east; and the Mount of Olives shall be split in two ... Then the Lord my God will come, and all the holy ones with him ... And there shall be continuous day ... not day and not night, for at evening time there shall be light ... And the Lord will become king over all the earth; on that day the Lord will be one and his name one. (Zechariah 14:4–9)

The time of the Church

Today, 2,000 years after the coming of the Messiah, we do not yet see the complete realisation of the era of reconciliation, of justice, of glory and of universal happiness foretold by the prophets. What the prophets describe there is the second coming of Christ. The time between the first and second coming, an interval the length of whose duration is unknown to us – a thousand years are like one single day for the Lord – that time is the time of the Church.

The messianic era inaugurated by the Paschal mystery of Christ and by the gift of the Spirit needs the collaboration of believers in order to be completed. It is up to us, in the power of the Spirit and with the hope that is founded on the visible manifestation of the tenderness and power of the Father, to begin to build from here below the Kingdom of God, kingdom of justice, of peace, of love, and to advance thus to meet the Lord who is coming. We can hasten the establishment of the Kingdom by the conversion of our heart and by our prayer. We are waiting for 'a new heaven and a new earth, where justice shall reside'. So Peter says:

> While you are waiting for these things, strive to be found by him at peace, without spot or blemish. (2 Peter 3:14)

Or, as John says:

> Abide in [Christ], so that when he is revealed we may have confidence and not be put to shame before him at his coming. (1 John 2:28)

The premonitory signs of the second coming

Jesus himself spoke of the last times and described certain signs, all quite catastrophic, which would allow us to recognise them. The language is that of the apocalyptic genre, highly symbolical. It is difficult to discern the real events evoked, apart from the destruction of Jerusalem described from near at hand.

Christ speaks clearly of his second coming. He takes up again the vision of Daniel: 'Then they will see the Son of Man coming in a cloud with power and great glory' (Luke 21:27).

The signs of that day are the destruction of the Temple in Jerusalem (this occurred in AD 70, and is the foreground of the prophecy); the coming of false prophets, wars, famines and earthquakes; the persecution of Christians, and failure of love and faith. Nevertheless, the Gospel will be proclaimed in the whole world, and 'after this' (as Paul himself says in Romans 11:26) 'Israel will be saved as well'. The mystery of the Jewish people, still waiting for the Messiah, is not as extraneous as we tend to think to the mystery of the waiting Church. And the final sign is the coming of Antichrist, the blasphemer who imitates God with his signs of great power.

There will be a definitive struggle between good and evil, between Christ and Satan. But Christ has already gained the victory by his death and resurrection. All that remains is to manifest it.

> The Lord Jesus will destroy him [the Antichrist] with the breath of his mouth, annihilating him by the manifestation of his coming. (2 Thessalonians 2:8)

Are these signs present in today's world? At every epoch some people have thought they discerned them in contemporary happenings, so great is the part played by catastrophes and the struggle between good and evil in human history. The Lord wills it so in order to give us the merit of the struggle. What is essential for us, however, is to accept the truth of the present human condition, and to prepare ourselves to fight with courage and perseverance in the absolute faith that the victory will be given us precisely through our participation in the sufferings and death of Christ. The servant will not follow any other way but that of his Master.

Let us not lose time in futile speculations. The Lord cut them short by saying categorically: 'But about that day and hour no one knows, neither the angels of heaven, nor the Son, but only the Father' (Matthew 24:36).

Vigilance
What counts for us is our attitude. The Gospel indicates well what it should be: 'Keep awake therefore, for you do not know on what day your Lord is coming' (Matthew 24:42).

> 'Be on your guard so that your hearts are not weighed down with dissipation and drunkenness and the worries of this life, and that day does not catch you unexpectedly like

a trap . . . Be alert at all times, praying that you may have the strength to escape all these things that will take place, and to stand before the Son of Man.' (Luke 21:34–36)

On the feast of St Bruno we read a remarkable text:

'Be dressed for action and have your lamps lit; be like those who are waiting for their master to return from the wedding banquet, so that they may open the door for him as soon as he comes and knocks. Blessed are those slaves whom the master finds alert when he comes; truly I tell you, he will fasten his belt and have them sit down to eat, and he will come and serve them.' (Luke 12:35–37)

What an extraordinary promise! Vigilance, sobriety, continual prayer – are they not the monk's trade?

Hidden presence

There is a mysterious dialectic between the first coming and the second. Jesus himself, facing the questioning of the Pharisees who wanted to know when the Kingdom of God was coming, pointed it out.

[Jesus] answered: 'The kingdom of God is not coming with things that can be observed; nor will they say, "Look, here it is!" or "There it is!" For, in fact, the kingdom of God is among you.'

Then he said to the disciples, 'The days are coming when you will long to see one of the days of the Son of Man, and you will not see it. They will say to you, "Look there!" or "Look here!" Do not go, do not set off in pursuit. For as the lightning flashes and lights up the sky from one side to the other, so will the Son of man be in his day. But first he must endure much suffering and be rejected by this generation.' (Luke 17:20–25)

Christ has come, and he remains present among us, in the Church (above all by the sacraments), in humanity with which he has entered into solidarity, and in the gift of the Spirit by which he penetrates the heart and is active there. On the other hand, he will come. There will be the Parousia, the return of Christ in glory at the end of time. There is not a simple discontinuity between the two. The period of the Church and the Spirit prepares and shapes beforehand the Parousia and the judgement. Eternity penetrates time. Eternity will be what we make it, here and now. Our ephemeral acts carry a weight of eternity; here below we build the city of God that will last for ever.

It is too simplistic to imagine our time as a line which advances point by point to come to an end one day. Then eternity would begin, more or less unconsciously imagined as an endless line. That is false, of course. Eternity is not the infinite prolongation of our created time. It is a totally different reality, which belongs to God's world and to the mystery of his being 'tota simul', that is a unique, perfect act. There is a presence of eternity in our time, as there is a presence of God to created being. How to convey that presence in terms of liberty (each act of liberty derives from the created and from eternity), of judgement and of Parousia, I do not know – but it exists. The Lord contented himself with telling us what we need to do in our temporal life. That is the essential.

The surprise element of the Lord's coming derives, therefore, not only from our ignorance of the day, but also from the hidden character of the presence of Christ among us. 'Have I been with you all this time, Philip, and you still do not know me?' (John 14:9). Shall we also say on the last day:

> 'Lord, when was it that we saw you hungry and gave you food, or thirsty and gave you something to drink? When was it that we saw you a stranger and welcomed you, or naked and gave you clothing? . . .' And the king will answer them: 'Truly I tell you, just as you did it to one of the least of these who are members of my family, you did it to me.' (Matthew 25:37–40)

The coming of the Bridegroom
The parable of the ten virgins also insists on the necessity to keep awake, to have our lamps full of the oil of effective charity.

How terrible it will be to hear that because we have forgotten God, God has forgotten us in turn: 'Truly I tell you, I do not know you.' But the parable also tells us that he who is coming, although formidable in so far as he judges, is also the Bridegroom of our soul. He is coming to consummate an intimate union already inaugurated by the gift of grace, but veiled in this life. Even in this life the Lord visits our heart, now and again unites with it, gives it a foretaste of that which will be the happiness of complete union. But often, it is in the murmur of a gentle breeze that he manifests himself. On our part, a great attention and the availability of a pure heart are necessary. Expectancy is the vital milieu of the contemplative, the expectancy of desire, of love. Expectancy at times in the dark, which hardly knows any more what it is expecting, but which waits all the same. Will he come? Has he come?

The Spirit and the bride say, 'Come' . . .
'Surely I am coming soon.'
Amen. Come, Lord Jesus!   (Revelation 22:17, 20)

3

John the Baptist

'Blessed is anyone who takes no offence at me.'
(Matthew 11:6)

Our churches are dedicated to John the Baptist and the Blessed
Virgin. Communities of solitaries, we spontaneously look
towards the Virgin who conceived the Eternal Word in the
silence of faith, and towards the rugged solitary set like a sen-
tinel on the threshold of the Kingdom of God. And yet Jesus
says, at least partly directed at John: 'Blessed is anyone who
takes no offence at me,' that is to say 'who will not stumble
because of me'. We know that, according to the Bible, 'scandal'
is not a bad example, nor an outrageous act, but etymologically
an obstacle, a trap, a stumbling-block which makes one fall
(Romans 9:33).

Our knowledge of John's first years is uncertain enough. He
withdrew into the desert from his youth. Did he belong to the
monastery of Qumram? We do not know it with certainty, but
it is certain that he began his mission on the banks of the
Jordan near enough to Qumram, where he administered a
purifying bath, and that he relied on a prophecy of Isaiah which
the Qumram community used in an analogous way, in applying
it to themselves: 'In the wilderness prepare the way of the Lord,
make straight in the desert a highway for our God' (Isaiah
40:3).

In any case, if John had come under the influence of
Qumram, he quickly went beyond its narrow, sectarian point
of view. He felt entrusted with a special mission: that of
announcing the nearness of the Kingdom of God in the person
of 'the One who is to come' (Matthew 11:3; Isaiah 40:10). He
calls to conversion not only a few chosen ones, but everybody,

the soldiers, the publicans, the prostitutes, in a simple, unpolished address. His baptism is the sign of a conversion which is realised in the conduct of daily life; it is administered once, and is not repeated in the pursuit of a legal, external purity.

Every monk likes this austere, simple, vigorous, humble man. His voice bears the vitality of years of silence, solitude and prayer. Effaced in front of his transparent message, John *is* a voice. A man of God, he looks at everything with the eyes of faith, he refuses to temporise with the mentality of the world, he does not hesitate to take the king to task for his bad life. He knows how to read the signs of the times correctly, and to see there the hour of God. He alone recognises in the obscure Nazarene 'the One who is to come', the Messiah.

WHAT WAS JOHN EXPECTING?

John was on the threshold of the Gospel. That threshold was not crossed without difficulty. It was not easy for John to accept that Jesus was the one he was expecting. He had pointed him out, God had given him the conviction that Jesus was the Messiah (Matthew 4:13–17); but afterwards, the manner in which Jesus fulfilled his mission confused him; it did not correspond to John's hopes. In his own person John summed up the expectation of the Old Testament with all the ardour of the prophetic tradition. But if there is a continuity between the Old and New Testaments, there is also a rupture. Christ makes the prefigurations and the figures of the Old Testament a reality, but he goes beyond them, and he invites those who believe in him to go beyond them. The failure of his ministry testifies to the difficulty of that 'going beyond' for the majority of the Jews. John was not an exception. Uneasy, from his prison he sends someone to ask Christ: 'Are you the one who is to come or are we to wait for another?' (Matthew 11:3). What a question on the lips of the one whose mission was none other than to be a voice to announce the Messiah! One senses the agitation of John in his obscure dungeon, awaiting death. Was he wrong? Was everything an illusion, vanity? His life, his word and his death?

What exactly was John expecting? He had said it clearly:

> 'I baptize you with water for repentance, but one who is
> more powerful than I is coming after me; I am not worthy
> to carry his sandals. He will baptize you with the Holy
> Spirit and fire.' (Matthew 3:11)

It is power which characterises the One who is to come. One
understands why, if one looks at the oracle of Isaiah 40, in
which John had recognised the definition of his own mission:
'A voice cries out, "In the wilderness prepare the way of the
Lord"' (Isaiah 40:3). The sequel announced: 'See, the Lord
God comes with might, and his arm rules for him' (40:10).
And read the magnificent description in 40:12–31 of the divine
greatness: Creator and master of all, the Lord can break the
oppressors and raise up the oppressed once again. One finds
the same affirmations in Malachi 3:1 which is applied equally
to the mission of John (Matthew 11:10): 'See, I am sending
my messenger to prepare the way before me.' The messenger
will be followed by the Lord in person.

> But who can endure the day of his coming, and who can
> stand when he appears? For he is like a refiner's fire and
> like fullers' soap; he will sit as a refiner and purifier of
> silver, and he will purify the sons of Levi ... (Malachi
> 3:2–3)

So one is not surprised that John should have precise ideas
about the manner in which that divine power is going to manifest itself.

> 'His winnowing-fork is in his hand, and he will clear his
> threshing-floor and will gather his wheat into the granary;
> but the chaff he will burn with unquenchable fire.'
> (Matthew 3:12)

The baptism in the Holy Spirit and the fire will be a destroying
bath. John sees in 'the One who is to come' the redoubtable
Judge who will eradicate with the unquenchable fire all the
sinners who have not repented of their sins and changed their
conduct before it is too late. John regards himself as entrusted

with preparing Israel for the terrible judgement, with helping them to escape the eternal punishment which threatens them. 'Even now the axe is lying at the root of the trees' (Matthew 3:10). But the manner in which Jesus fulfils his mission does not correspond at all to that idea and arouses John's astonishment.

JESUS' REPLY TO JOHN

To John's question Jesus replies in words chosen on purpose to recall the messianic oracles of the second part of the book of Isaiah. His works are the ones by which the Messiah was meant to manifest himself.

> The spirit of the Lord God is upon me,
>   because the Lord has anointed me;
> he has sent me to bring good news to the oppressed,
>   to bind up the broken-hearted.
>
> (Isaiah 61:1, cf. Matthew 11:4–5)

Jesus does not content himself with affirming that he is the Messiah: he gives his proofs. But at the same time, he invites John to envisage the role of the Messiah under a quite different aspect to that which had held his attention. Nothing of the prophetic intuition of the greatness, the holiness and the justice of God is to be abandoned; but that intuition is to be completed by the revelation of other aspects of the divine conduct already present in the Old Testament, which will be given first place and be infinitely deepened by the revelation which Jesus brings. The God of holy anger who, all things considered, corresponded to the idea that human beings can form of God and his justice, must give way to a God of Love, infinitely more disconcerting.

Christ foresees that his reply to John could disappoint him. Instead of the 'Strong One' deploying the avenging power of God's anger against sinners, Jesus presents himself as the manifestation of the Lord's merciful tenderness towards the poor and all those who suffer. The contrast is great! Will John manage to accept the revelation of love which is made in humility and weakness? His very virtues will be an obstacle for him: his vigour, his austerity, his zeal. He claims a strong, redoubtable God, and Jesus presents himself as gentle and humble of heart, and happy to bestow his forgiveness. Jesus reveals that the omnipotence of God is the omnipotence of love – the infinite gift of self, of gratuitousness, of forgiveness; the power which shows what it is capable of in assuming the weakness of a human being and his death.

John's test finds a good illustration in the story of Jonah. He also had been entrusted with a message of anger: God is going to destroy Nineveh! But Nineveh repents and God forgives her. Jonah's prophecy does not come to pass. Jonah gets angry (Jonah 4:1). Had he not been right to want to escape from his mission? 'I knew that you are a gracious God and merciful, slow to anger, and abounding in steadfast love, and ready to relent from punishing' (Jonah 4:2). God never makes up his mind to strike!

STUMBLING BLOCKS

Nearer to Christ, one remembers the reaction of Peter, who, after having professed the sovereign dignity of Jesus at Caesarea Philippi, is scandalised at the idea of the sufferings which Jesus announces (Matthew 16:22–23). It is really difficult to receive the revelation of the powerless God, which Jesus brings. On this occasion it is Jesus who is scandalised (still in the biblical sense). 'Get behind me, Satan!' he says to Peter. 'You are a stumbling-block to me, for you are setting your mind not on divine things but on human things' (Matthew 16:23).

Even his intimate disciples (but they were first the disciples of John the Baptist, let us not forget!) James and that John, who will one day sing a magnificent song to love – even they, after having listened to the Master and lived with him for a long time, react like John the Baptist against the refusal of a town in Samaria to receive Jesus: 'Lord, do you want us to command fire to come down from heaven and consume them?' (Luke 9:54). In all truth, they did not know of what spirit they were!

We, to whom the Gospel is familiar since childhood, we

cannot imagine the religious upheaval which the preaching of a God who wants to deal with sinners represented for the contemporaries of Jesus. Every page of the Gospel shows the scandal, the agitation, the upheaval which Jesus provokes by calling to salvation precisely the sinners, instead of exterminating them, and by opposing to every pretension of human justice before God a religion of faith and gratuitous love.

Unceasingly he was asked the reason for that incomprehensible attitude, and unceasingly, above all in his parables, he gave the same reply: God is like that. God is the father who goes to meet his prodigal son; he is the shepherd who rejoices because his sheep is found again; he is the host who invites the poor and the beggars to his table. God feels more joy for the one sinner who does penance than for the ninety-nine righteous persons. He is the God of the little ones and the hopeless; his goodness and his mercy are without limit. God is like that.

THE KINGDOM OF GOD

There is no reason to think that John the Baptist did not fully accept the answer Jesus addressed to him. It does not seem correct to understand Matthew 11:11 in that sense. It is evident that Jesus' intention is to praise John, not to exclude him from the Kingdom. 'Truly I tell you, among those born of women no one has arisen greater than John the Baptist.' That is to say, if one considers human beings in their earthly condition, in the achievements of human strength, asceticism, or virtue, the first place goes to John; but compared to the privileges which participation in the Kingdom confers, all that is nothing: 'Yet the least in the kingdom of heaven is greater than he' (Matthew 11:11).

The opposition bears on two orders of grandeur; that of this world and that of the Kingdom: Jesus wants to emphasise the absolute superiority of the second. The affirmation does not at all imply that John would not also be called to enjoy those privileges of the world to come. The attention does not stop with John; starting with him, it rises up to the consideration of the Kingdom which is to come and the totally new conditions of existence which it brings to those who will share in it.

In order to enter the Kingdom, a new birth is needed, so radical that it can only be a gratuitous gift of God. We must actively co-operate in it, be converted with all our heart, but all the time knowing that our effort itself is also a gift of God. We do not take possession of the Kingdom by our strength or our virtue. We receive it by faith and trust, we respond to the merciful love of God by our love.

It is so simple and so great that we, the grown-ups who take ourselves to be something, have a great deal of difficulty in really believing it. The Kingdom reverses our whole scale of values. Our poverty is our wealth (Matthew 5:1); our weakness, our strength (2 Corinthians 12:10); our most fruitful activity is to suffer the gentle violence of the divine love. In order to win, one must lose. In order to live, die.

It is the logic of love. The Kingdom is the Kingdom of love. To be at one's ease in that marvellous land, one must have the simplicity of a child, the irrevocable humility, the trustful dependence of a child, the joy, the heart of a child – of a child born of God, child of the Father.

'Truly I tell you, unless you change and become like children, you will never enter the kingdom of heaven. Whoever becomes humble like this child is the greatest in the kingdom of heaven.' (Matthew 18:3–4)

4

Jesus and John

We have meditated on the figure of John the Baptist presented by the Synoptics, whose texts are read during the second week of Advent. The gospels of the third week also speak of John the Baptist, but as seen by John, the fourth Evangelist.

In this Gospel, John the Baptist is the witness: he renders testimony to Jesus at the beginning of his public mission; it is the disciples of John who are the first to follow Jesus. As Jesus comes to the foreground, John slips away. His last word in this Gospel is: 'He must increase, but I must decrease' (John 3:30).

John is the ideal apostle. 'Apostle', in Greek, means he who is sent to announce another. He exists essentially in reference to the one who is to come. His role is to warn the people, to summon them to purify themselves in order to receive the divine presence which is approaching, which is already there in a hidden way.

Not that he should be a colourless sign. On the contrary, John's personality is clearly marked, and of great strength. A great ascetic come out of the desert, bearer of a mission and a message, he knows how to make enthusiastic disciples and to impress even the religious authorities whom he fiercely criticises. There were those in the first century who venerated John the Baptist to the point of placing him above Jesus and regarding him as the Messiah. So we understand the humility of John better – he does not allow the attention to be fixed on him.

The Gospel text is probably influenced by the necessity of replying to those sectarians. The baptism of Jesus by John is not directly described in this Gospel, and the pre-eminence of Jesus is underlined, seen in all his depth as Word of God.

> There was a man sent from God, whose name was John. He came as a witness to testify to the light, so that all might believe through him. He himself was not the light, but he came to testify to the light. The true light, which enlightens everyone, was coming into the world. (John 1:6–9)

John is not the light. 'I am not the Christ, nor the Prophet announced by Moses, nor Elijah who is to return according to Jewish expectation.' 'Then, who are you?' 'A voice,' he answers, 'the voice of one crying out in the wilderness: "Make straight the way of the Lord" ' (1:23). A voice which speaks a Word that is not his but the Word of God himself. The Word that is the light of all.

John is the clear glass which allows the light to pass through without distorting it. That is his poverty and his greatness. And nevertheless, he differed from Jesus in character (see Matthew 11:18–19). The ascetic and his intransigent strength were necessary to point out the light; but he is not the final word of God, which appears on the infinitely more mysterious face of love.

Augustine sums up John's role thus, attributing these words to him:

> I listen; it is he who speaks (3:29).
> I am enlightened; he is the light (1:6–9).
> I am the ear; he is the Word (3:29).

John belongs to the category of symbol: what he does is only symbolic and must be transcended. John baptises in water, for the purification of hearts. There will come the One on whom the Spirit of God will descend, in whom the Spirit will dwell. Thus the anointed one, the Christ, will baptise for a new birth in God. This is the reality which the Baptist could only invoke and signify.

But this reality is still hidden. Jesus is present as 'the One you do not know'. John knows how to recognise him by the sign of the Spirit: 'He on whom you see the Spirit descend and remain' (1:33) – not rest in passing, but remain, abiding in a stable and permanent way.

Jesus, among us as the one we do not know. John, to cry for us: 'Purify your hearts. Look! He is there, very near to you.' 'The word is near you, on your lips and in your heart' (Romans 10:8; Deuteronomy 30:14).

We will know how to recognise and receive Christ in so far as we walk under the impulse of the Spirit. We know the signs of the Spirit of the Lord: love, joy, peace, patience, kindness, goodness, trustfulness, gentleness, self-control – the works of the light. Christ is there. We also know the signs of the evil spirit: fornication, gross indecency and sexual irresponsibility, idolatry and sorcery, feuds and wrangling, jealousy, bad temper and quarrels, disagreements, factions, envy, etc. (Galatians 5:17–25) – the works of darkness, where the Spirit of darkness dwells.

Our look is in terms of the purity of our heart. How many times have I failed to recognise Christ, have I passed by him, eyes blinded by my egoism, my passions and my cupidities? Also by my foolishness: like the Jews, am I waiting for something extraordinary, spectacular, announced with a show of strength, when Christ walks close to me in the hidden mystery of a 'banal' humanity – banal, to the casual glance of the inattentive, but full of the divine for the one who knows how to look.

Like a child: one must welcome the Kingdom of God, Christ in his humanity, my brother and my sister in the beauty of their hope, like a child. 'Just as you did it to one of the least of these who are members of my family, you did it to me' (Matthew 25:40). Is that Christmas, here and now? The mysterious gestation of Christ in my heart, in my love?

John points out Jesus, calling him 'the Lamb of God, who takes away the sin of the world' (1:29). The ascetic summoned him, prepared the ground for him; only the sacrifice of the love which gives all truly reconciles with God. Now John can disappear. Some of his disciples leave him to follow Jesus. Jesus begins to baptise and the crowds go to him. If not John, at least his disciples are not happy. John's reply is magnificent:

'No one can receive anything except what has been given from heaven. You yourselves are my witnesses that I said, "I am not the Messiah, but I have been sent ahead of him." ' (John 3:27–28)

To each his grace, his role, in God's plan. The essential thing is to fulfil it. The characteristic of the person is to realise oneself in giving oneself, in actually losing oneself. The pointing finger directs the gaze not to himself, but to Christ. If the gaze should rest on himself, he is unfaithful to his own nature. That is, however, the temptation of every apostle!

But John transcends those perspectives with an outburst of the heart.

'He who has the bride is the bridegroom. The friend of the bridegroom, who stands and hears him, rejoices greatly at the bridegroom's voice. For this reason my joy has been fulfilled. He must increase, but I must decrease.' (John 3:29–30)

More than an apostle, the friend, whose joy is Jesus' joy. To rejoice in the happiness of one's friend as one's own – that is genuine friendship. John the ascetic must have loved Jesus humanly and profoundly.

The beautiful joy of a disinterested love: that he may grow greater, that he may be recognised and loved; that I may grow smaller, getting out of the way. The voice which resounded, so virile and so strong, in the desert, communicated the Word. Then it is silent. It returns to the silence from which it was born; a silence inhabited by the Word made flesh in John's heart; a silence fully given over to the intimate joy of love given; a gift which will be sealed by the sacrifice of life in Herod's dungeon. It is to Christ's joy that John the ascetic wants to lead us. It is for that reason that, in the readings of this week and in the Introit of the Mass, we celebrate that joy which Christ brings us and which no one can ever take from us.

Rejoice in the Lord always; again I will say, Rejoice. Let your gentleness be known to everyone. The Lord is near. (Philippians 4:4–5)

THE ONE AMONG YOU WHOM YOU DO NOT KNOW

One of the lessons of the Advent liturgy is that history has a meaning. Not only sacred history, but also the whole of human history, and more particularly our own history, are a series of events in which we detect the hand of God revealed.

In the events which led to the birth of Christ, there were not so many things that stood out clearly from ordinary life. They happened almost unnoticed. By making us see in them the action of God, the Word of God invites us, at the same time, to open our eyes to that action of God in the more or less simple events of each of our own lives, and thus to discover their hidden meaning. Each one of us is caught up in a history which is the right side of something we all see only on the reverse.

To be sure, the Bible is the account of the perpetual repetition of a history of troubles and tears, of expectations and lapses of hope. It teaches us, however, that history has a meaning. It affirms that meaning in the most paradoxical way there is, through a helpless child, born in a poor crib, in a little out-of-the-way village. It affirms for us that there where the forces of death seem to prevail, true life announces itself.

One of our difficulties is that we do not see the whole; we only see the minute part of history represented by our own tiny life. The place that this occupies in the great tapestry of God's global plan escapes us, as well as its true significance and its value.

We believe that all things work together for the good of those who love God, that his providence encompasses and governs all, down to the smallest detail, but we do not see it, above all in our moments of obscurity. At best, we grasp something of the coherence of God's providence in our life well after the event, in a backward look at some key moment of our existence. But our faith assures us that the Lord is very near us at each moment of our journey, even if, often, we do not recognise him.

Since the Incarnation, he has bound himself up with our

human condition, he is near in all the folds of our history, in our moments of weakness and sin too. He is there, a presence of mercy, of pardon and of grace; humbly offering us from alongside us, like a brother, his love and the gift of his life. A divine gift, for his life is the life of God.

That is the true Christmas present – the others are only its reflections and symbols. And that is the source of a joy which no one, nor any trouble, nor any event, whatever it may be, can take from us.

Once again we return to the words of the Introit for this third Sunday of Advent – words that we can *always* make our own:

> Rejoice in the Lord always; again I will say, Rejoice. Let your gentleness be known to everyone. The Lord is near. Do not worry about anything, but in everything by prayer and supplication with thanksgiving let your requests be made known to God. And the peace of God, which surpasses all understanding, will guard your hearts and your minds in Christ Jesus. (Philippians 4:4–7)

That peace and that joy in the Lord, I wish you all this Christmas.

5

Receptivity

I speak little of the Blessed Virgin. It is not that I am indifferent to her, but because there are things so simple in their beauty that one can only impair them by speaking of them – at least if one is not a great poet, for poetry has the wisdom not to want to understand and describe, but to suggest and evoke by its symbols and music the mystery of beauty which always remains beyond words.

But this time of Advent is a preparation for the coming of the incarnate Word. We should open ourselves to the action of the Spirit who will give birth to Christ in our hearts. In that case, we instinctively turn towards Mary in whom this mystery was realised in its fullness. So we will speak about her, but with much reserve. The presence of a woman is all the more precious as it is full of reserve, of delicacy, of attentive transparency, as it is pure presence: hands of peace and tenderness on the forehead of humanity.

Each one forms for himself a personal idea of God, and also of the Virgin. In both cases, these ideas risk being strongly influenced by the projection of our desire and our personalities. Let us try to place ourselves at the school of the Word of God, without adding or subtracting anything. That mode of action is, I believe, the wisest and is the nearest to the spirit of the Church.

Today I will only speak of one thing concerning the Blessed Virgin: her receptivity to God's action in the Annunciation scene, according to the Gospel of St Luke 1:26–38.

A young girl, probably aged from twelve to fourteen years, the age of Jewish engagements in that poor village of Nazareth in Galilee, was promised in marriage to a carpenter named Joseph; this young girl was called Mary. One day, she was visited by a messenger from God, an angel who, speaking to her, gave her this beautiful name: Kecharitomene. This Greek name is hard to translate; it means 'You-who-have-God's-favour', in the sense in which someone finds favour in the eyes of a king or a lover. We know that, for the Bible, the name designates the essence of the person. God's first word about Mary is a word of favour, the initiative of a sovereign and gratuitous love. 'Rejoice!' Mary, you are loved by God, in you appears the dawn of that so longed-for intervention of God in history for the salvation of humankind. 'The Lord is with you.'

The young girl, who obviously is not used to supernatural visits, is very upset by this irruption of the divine mystery into her life; she does not understand. The angel, whose kind concern can be seen, hastens to reassure her: 'Do not be afraid, Mary; you have won God's favour.' That favour is going to take a concrete and precise form. The whole scene unfolds with solemn dignity: God respects the young girl's freedom, replies to her legitimate difficulties in understanding, awaits her consent. He reveals the future as an invitation to that which can only be realised by Mary's 'fiat'.

'And now you will conceive in your womb and bear a son, and you will name him Jesus.' The name of Jesus is not explained, as it is in Matthew 1:21 ('God saves'), but the extraordinary character of this son is clearly indicated: 'He will be great, and will be called the Son of the Most High, and the Lord God will give to him the throne of his ancestor David. He will reign over the house of Jacob for ever, and of his kingdom there will be no end' (1:32–33). These words of the angel draw their inspiration from several messianic passages of the Old Testament and designate the child as the expected Messiah.

Before this promise which ought to have dazzled the lowly country girl, Mary appears neither excited nor elated. She endeavours to understand, to situate this promise in her real world. Instinctively, she looks towards the realisation of the promise, which shows her will to receive it, and immediately she sees the difficulty: 'How can this come about, since I know not man?' In this context, 'to know' means, in the biblical sense, to have conjugal relations. Mary is engaged to Joseph, she is not living with him yet and their union has not been consummated. Mary is a virgin. The word used indicates her present state, but it is difficult to see the meaning of the objection if it does not also express the intention of remaining a virgin. Without this there would be no problem for a young wife to have the promised child in the normal way. One must therefore assume that Mary has the will to remain a virgin, a will put in concrete form, perhaps, in a vow to God (the text does not specify). What was the meaning of that resolution? A Jewish woman considered the fact of remaining childless a great misfortune, indeed, a divine punishment. Celibacy had very little honour, except in the rather restricted Jewish sect of the Essenes. Their attitude resulted, apparently, not only from religious fervour, but also from dualistic ideas about created values and from an obsession with legal impurity.

It is not at all evident that Mary shared those ideas. All that the Gospel tells us inclines us to situate her rather in another religious context, that of the 'anawim'. In these 'poor of the Lord' one finds the purest flame of Old Testament piety. They are the genuine 'remnant' of the chosen people, the most faithful disciples of the prophets. People of a simple, living piety, materially poor and spiritually humble, putting all their trust in God, and living in the fervent expectation of the coming of God who will save his people, as the prophets announced. Their humility exerts a gentle violence on God, and their empty hands are fully ready to receive the generosity of his goodness.

> This poor soul cried, and was heard by the Lord,
>   and was saved from every trouble . . .
> O taste and see that the Lord is good;
>   happy are those who take refuge in him.
>
> (Psalm 34:6, 8)

It is to these poor in spirit that Jesus himself will announce the good news of the Father's love: the kingdom of heaven is theirs (Matthew 5:2).

Their spiritual accent reappears in the mouth of 'the humble handmaid' of the Lord (Luke 1:48), in her poverty, her simplicity, her total self-surrender to God. It seems that Mary's resolution to remain a virgin is the expression of her total receptivity to the awaited coming of the Kingdom of God, her total adherence to God. This non-conforming resolution could not have been made lightly. It implies a surprising maturity in this young girl of between twelve and fourteen years, and the full agreement of her fiancé Joseph. So God gave her the firm conviction that her virginity would remain intact.

And now God says to her: You will be a mother! Is God contradicting himself? Was she mistaken? The behaviour which embodied her expectation of God, her receptivity to his coming, her virginity, seems to be in contradiction with the means God chooses to fulfil that expectation: her motherhood. But that is only a contradiction for human reason. For God, everything is possible, everything becomes a way. Mary's virginity is destined to be fruitful. How? 'The Holy Spirit will come upon you, and the power of the Most High will overshadow you; therefore the child to be born will be holy; he will be called Son of God' (1:35). The term 'Son of God' indicates the Messiah, but joined to the term 'holy' which in St Luke's thinking marks the exclusive adherence to God, it already opens on to the mystery of Christ's divine sonship. It is the Spirit who effects God's creative work at the beginning (Genesis 1:2; Psalm 104:30). It is the Spirit who effects the investiture of the Messiah who will bring salvation to humankind (Isaiah 11:1–6). It is the Spirit who effects the conception of Mary's Son. Jesus, born of the action of the Holy, will be eminently holy.

Mary is the first to whom God gave the hundredfold already here below. This hundredfold for her is the birth of the Messiah, Son of God. That which she relinquished, she finds again at God's level, where she is established.

God himself gives her the conviction that she must assume the most embodied dimension of her womanhood, which she relinquished for God. But this will be in such a manner that the one who will be born of her will be fully 'spiritual', that is to say, the work of the Spirit, while at the same time being fully human. She must actively consent to the mysterious action of the Spirit in her. The power of the Most High covers her with its shadow. One cannot see clearly in shadow, even when it is the shadow of Love (Song of Solomon 2:3). It is to faith and trust that the promise invites her, not to clear understanding. Like Moses, Mary must enter into the luminous cloud which God inhabits (Exodus 13:22; 19:16), a cloud which reveals his presence while hiding his face. She must abandon her own project of virginity for God, in order that God may fulfil it in an eminent but hidden way, in the fruitfulness of spiritual and human motherhood.

That must have been very difficult. It is easier to be converted from our sins than to abandon our generosities, our projects of good will into which we have fully put ourselves. They seem to establish our security before God. That is where their profound weakness lies – they can close us to God's utter generosity, and to ours in response. It is vitally important to have this receptivity to the unexpected, to the unknown, to the mystery, when God invites us to it. Otherwise we risk enclosing God's action within the narrow limits of our human expectations. In practice, this receptivity is arduous. It implies great discernment in listening to God's voice and a great liberty in following it. When it is a question of something that goes outside the normal channels, the divine invitation is not at all clear or easy to grasp. It is in our nature to exclude what we do not understand, to be deaf to what is beyond us. To glimpse an unusual invitation and to respond to it demands a radical surrender to God in faith and trust, demands a great humility. Remember that the result of the divine intervention in Mary's case must have been disconcerting for the people around her who knew about it. Joseph's reaction proves that.

God knows well the difficulty of what he is asking of Mary. So he gives her a sign to support her faith: the birth of John the Baptist, precursor of Jesus, a contrasting sign, since the precursor is born of aged parents, like Isaac in the past (Genesis 18:14). 'Nothing will be impossible with God' (1:37).

Mary does not hesitate any more. Composed, she expresses her total and active receptivity in the simplest terms: 'Here am I, the servant of the Lord; let it be with me according to your word' (1:38). Her reception of God's Word is total; in a unique way, with all her heart and all her body, she conceives and gives birth to the Word made flesh.

This birth of Christ is the principle and the model of his birth in the heart of each one of us. We are asked to receive him with the receptivity of a faith which does not set down conditions nor limits; with the simplicity and confidence which expect everything from God, to whom nothing is impossible; with the supple audacity of a humility which does not settle down comfortably in the realisation of its good will, nor in its own wisdom, but which immerses itself in the mystery of God and lets itself be carried by God's folly, on to unforeseen paths, towards unknown objectives.

In the divine adventure there is neither past nor future, there is only the 'fiat' of the present moment which makes us enter into that eternity of God where the Word is begotten by the Father, to return to him in the impetuosity of love. This same love forms Christ in us and carries us with him towards the Father.

This eternal birth takes place in the inmost depths of our heart. Let us try to enter into this Advent by the recollection of a profound prayer and by the receptivity of a complete freedom for God. Let us be vigilant, and ready at each moment, in each action, to receive the invitation of the Word, to let ourselves be led by the Spirit in all our actions and judgements. Thus, Christ will be born in us, little by little, more so every day, until he reaches his full stature (Ephesians 4:13). With Christ, in Christ, will be born love which is his will in all things, and his joy, the fruit of his Spirit in us. Perhaps we will be able one day to sing with Mary, with the same wonder before the unhoped-for outcome of the divine work in us:

My soul magnifies the Lord,
    and my spirit rejoices in God my Saviour . . .
        the Mighty One has done great things for me,
    and holy is his name.

(Luke 1:47, 49)

CHRISTMAS

6

Christmas Joy

'Do not be afraid; for see – I am bringing you news of great joy for all the people: to you is born this day in the city of David a Saviour, who is the Messiah, the Lord.'

(Luke 2:10–11)

One ought to speak joyfully about joy, sing it like the angels on the night of Jesus' birth. Since I have not the voice of an angel, let us at least gather their message into our heart in imitation of the silent Mary. It is good news that the angels sing, a great joy for the whole people, for all the world. The time for fear is over, do not be afraid. The messianic times have arrived. He who was to come is in the midst of us. He is born to us – a Saviour who is Christ the Lord. He comes to save us from sin, from evil and from death. He brings atonement and pardon. He offers us the free love of God and eternal life. He gives us his joy, a joy drawn from the inexhaustible fountain of the Father's infinite gift, a joy which gushes forth in us from the Father's heart, making us his children. Truly:

'Glory to God in the highest heaven,
   and on earth peace among those whom he favours!'

(Luke 2:14)

Let the whole earth exult before the salvation of the Lord;
the mountains, the rivers, the animals, the trees, the birds,
let everything glorify the Lord, for his mercy and love are
boundless. (Anonymous)

During this Christmas period, the psalms take on a very special density of meaning and lyrical ardour; the Liturgy makes every-thing sing, in making us sing.

In the Old Testament joy was regarded as the sign of a life which is blossoming out, the characteristic of the time of sal-vation and of eschatological peace. If Jesus revealed to us everything he heard from his Father, it is that we might thus be his friends and that his joy might be in us and that our joy might be perfect (John 15:11). The joy of communion, of friendship, the joy of sharing in such a strong life, his risen life, 'that joy no one will take from you', even if in this life it is accompanied by, indeed born of, sorrow (John 16:20–22). Joy generally does not grant an absence of combat: it is Paschal; so it is rather the heart of the combat, that which makes it possible and victorious beforehand. And our hearts? Are they fully joyful? Is there not a ground of sadness? Why? Christmas brings us joys, that is certain, but joy, do we know it? O men of little faith!

We remain too fastened to our fears, to our self-sufficiency, to our independence, to our pride, to our shoddy riches, to our cherished poverties, in short, to ourselves, to have the audacity of spiritual joy and to let ourselves open out to the measure of God's gift. Joy opens out, sadness closes one in. To be joyful, a certain self-forgetfulness is necessary, a loss of self in wonder. That is why the joy of the adult is so often stiff, that of the child so complete. Little by little the adult comes to place his joy in possessions, sometimes very material ones. But possessing belongs rather to the category of pleasure; to receive and to give, that is joy! And joy is always a gift, it always bears the stamp of gratuitousness, of festivity. Often, the adult does not know how to receive what is freely given in all simplicity, in the poverty filled with non-possession which alone gives access to true riches. In our consumer society people think that they can buy everything, possess everything. But we can only ever buy *things*. They are hunted out, they are accumulated. We may own a lot of them but find no joy in them, only insatiable pleasure and, ultimately, boredom. Joy, on the contrary, is the daughter of poverty, of gratuitousness, of the audacity of the life that lives and laughs in us.

The contemplative should have something of that wisdom of the child, of the child's capacity for giving, for surrender. 'O Bonitas' sang Bruno: a cry of wonder-struck joy. Some of us seem to believe that only 'serious' people are serious: it is obligatory that wisdom should wear clothes that are wholly correct, display a solemn gait and a frowning face. The businessman of *The Little Prince* is too busy counting and 'owning' the stars to look at their beauty and open his heart to their song. Let us be simple, let us not be afraid to be joyful.

But since we have lost the spontaneity of simplicity, let us go in search of it with the heavy steps of our reason.

Joy – what is it? It is the feeling we experience in becoming aware of the full blossoming of our life. There are always two elements: the blossoming of a capacity for life and the consciousness of that blossoming, a certain experimental consciousness of what is lived. And because our life is situated at different levels, physical, emotional, intellectual and spiritual, there exist for us different joys of very diverse qualities. The joy of eating well or of having good health is quite different from the joy of friendship. And the joy of friendship is quite different from that of contemplation. That joy will be the greatest, but not necessarily the most emotional. It comes from the blossoming of the highest life.

It is evident that these diverse joys are not always given simultaneously. The joy of friendship can go hand in hand with a feeling of sadness. It is easy to understand how Christian joy is born of the blossoming of Christ's life in us and of the coming to awareness of the presence of that life of love and divine knowledge, of that life of friendship with God, of our participation in the life of the Trinity. Christian joy is therefore the joy of Christ's presence in our heart and, through him, that of the whole personal mystery of God's love. It is inseparable from a deep faith and a real charity which give a certain knowledge, by sharing in the same nature, of the Life that dwells in us; it is greatly nourished by a life of interior and intimate prayer.

Christian joy is a spiritual joy, that is to say, the fruit of the Spirit. It reaches the deepest level of our being, there where our being is 'capax Dei', capable of receiving the communication of the divine and eternal life. So I call it joy, because it is the blossoming in us of God's joy, which is identical with his being.

Like being, joy is a gift, a gift which one must know how to accept, to which one must know how to surrender. The poverty that does not grab, the simplicity that renders itself transparent to the joy which Christ wants to live and love in us, the surrender that rids itself of a calculating self-security in order to sing the gratuitousness, the festiveness of God – those are the dispositions which give the joy of being.

Spiritual joy often overflows, lighting up our whole being, but not always. Christ himself could say: 'my soul is sorrowful to the point of death', he who was never separated from the joy of his Father.

As there is a source in the depths of my heart from which my being springs up, there is also one from which my joy, an eternal joy, springs up; in both cases the source is the same. We *are* a joy which too often does not know itself. I wish the chattering of our sadness would be silent – sadness never ceases to express itself – so that the silence might let joy go.

> While gentle silence enveloped all things . . .
> your all-powerful word leapt from heaven,
>> from the royal throne.
>>> (Wisdom 18:14, Introit of the Sunday after Christmas)

Whatever happens at other levels of my being, that joy is always there, in so far as I am linked to God in his grace. I can always rediscover that joy: it is enough to make a supernatural act of faith and love, to say in my heart, I want to believe, I want to love, whatever may be the obscurity in which I find myself at the psychological and emotional levels.

THE JOY OF MARY

Let us be guided by Mary in order to learn joy. We have so few words of hers. These words have great density because they carry an immense weight of silence. There is the 'fiat', the 'yes' by which Mary freely consents to the gift of God, to the gift God makes to her of himself, to the mysterious action of the

Holy Spirit by which Jesus is conceived in her. And Jesus is begotten in joy. Mary's heart is filled with elation, with the elation of a poor person who knows how to receive life.

'My soul magnifies the Lord,
    and my spirit rejoices in God my Saviour.'

(Luke 1:47)

This is a joy which, when shared, awakens joy in Elizabeth's heart.

The child in his mother's womb draws nourishment from her substance, builds himself from what she is; the mother lets him do it. It all happens in the silence of an intense symbiosis between two people. Mary is alone with her hidden child; for the child, his universe is Mary's womb.

Then the time comes when the Child emerges to enter into our world. It is the first separation that is going to allow him to be the One who is among us, for us. As it is said, Mary brings him into the world. And her joy is to give him. Her heart is full of a joy that is not at all diminished by having to give birth in such poor circumstances, in a stable, given shelter among animals, there being no room for them among their own kind.

But the child is a king, a poor king, a king twofold. The angels sing their wonder, announce the joy of his coming to those who are best disposed to receive him: the poor, the shepherds, and those who seek him along the paths of human wisdom, the Magi.

We have no word from Mary. She remains completely silent, she is engaged in protecting that little body which is so vulnerable, enfolding it in swaddling clothes and placing it in a manger. She is a mother, she has to devote herself to the duties of motherhood, while remaining united to her son in her heart. But now there is a face to face encounter, two people look at each other, the love becomes more personal, a love of friendship; soon the child's smile will answer hers.

But Mary still says nothing. She lets the shepherds and the Magi lay their tribute before her son. It is the angels who sing his glory. She herself preserves all these things, keeps them in her heart.

Who was this being born of her? Her heart knows of it more deeply than her intelligence can formulate. Mary does not speak of her son, she is not the Word, but his servant. She gives birth to Jesus by her whole being, she shows him by her presence, by her whole attitude; she serves him, looks at him; her silence speaks for her, speaks her love.

It will be so all her life. During the long peaceful years of Nazareth, her joy is the constant intimacy with Jesus, the life shared with the young man who grows before her eyes. He is her son and nevertheless one day in Jerusalem, when only just twelve years old, he says: 'Did you not know that I must be in my Father's house?' Jesus returns to Nazareth, life continues, but not as before. The stamp of the Father is on the child; to the joy of his intimacy is added a solemn note, of respect, before the mystery of his being.

In the dialectic of intimacy and separation, little by little, Jesus reveals himself to his mother – as to his disciples, as to us. Each time there is a deepening. One day he will go as far as radically relegating to second place the ties of blood that unite them. 'Whoever does the will of God is my brother and sister and mother' (Mark 3:35).

It is on the rock of the Father's will that their communion must henceforth be based and be made strong to the point where the final separation of a brutal death must be accepted. Where is your joy now, Mary? It is still there, still springing up from that ultimate level of your being, there where the 'yes' of your love and faith is repeated in silence, in a terrible solitude. Never were you so much a woman. In this way you become the mother of the Body of Christ, of us all. Solemn joy of a love that gives more than itself.

Love is stronger than death, joy stronger than sadness. The light of the Resurrection is going to inundate the space of Mary's faith and fill her with a joy that will have no end. Her assumption into heaven is only the manifestation of the plenitude of that joy which transforms and impregnates her whole being, including her body.

Mary does not leave one word about Jesus, no theology, no discourse. Her life is her word, her love, her knowledge, her total self-giving to God's will and to the hidden action of the Spirit in her, her joy, her poverty, the transparence of her purity.

That joy is Christ in her, it is Christ in us. I wish you that joy with all my heart.

We are responsible for our joy.

7

In the Beginning

A new year is beginning under the patronage of the Holy Mother of God, the 'year of grace' 1999. The expression is perhaps old-fashioned, but it is profoundly Christian. Since the coming of Christ, the whole of human history is under the sign of grace, the sign of the salvation offered to everyone. The year that is commencing presents itself to our faith as a gift of the Father's love. It will be, we know, governed by his providence and wisdom, the work of his eternal Word, a space open before our liberty in the Spirit. 'All things work together for good for those who love God' (Romans 8:28).

THE SPIRAL

Life follows a constant movement: days, months, seasons and years follow each other in accordance with a regular rhythm. Even our body cells die in order to renew themselves periodically. The ancients, above all the Greeks, understood the unfolding of time in the image of a circle: a circle closed upon itself, the eternal return.

> What has been is what will be,
>   and what has been done is what will be done;
>   there is nothing new under the sun . . .
> Vanity of vanities! All is vanity.
>
> (Ecclesiastes 1:9, 2)

One must not let oneself be fascinated by this disillusioned and paralysing fatalism. The Word of God gives us the key to history by revealing to us that it is directed towards a single end, the Parousia, the reign of God realised in its plenitude at the end of time. The idea of history is of a linear movement aiming at one single goal. The image of a spiral, however, allows us to incorporate the Greek intuition of the cyclical character of time. The spiral always traces the same curve, but not on the same plane. It rises (or descends) progressively. What makes the curve always the same is the weight of our nature, its determinisms, its 'material' laws. What makes the spiral rise (or descend) is our liberty, that spark of creative power that we have from God and that is more precious and of a different order than the whole material universe. It is our liberty, informed by faith, that permits us to project ourselves outside ourselves (*ec-stasis*), beyond our tiny ego buried in our individual nature, in a surge of love and hope, a miracle of endless new beginnings, the victory of spirit over matter. Let us try, on this first day of the year, to recollect ourselves, gather our strength again in order to launch ourselves into the new year, in the joy of our faith.

TO BEGIN AGAIN EVERY MORNING

To begin seems to be the prerogative of youth: spontaneity, freshness, a totally new vitality that is revealed and unfolds, the naivety of inexperience. To begin again is more difficult. The experienced knowledge of the limits, the memory of the failures, the hurts, the weariness of time, the burden of the flesh, all that weighs one down and cunningly whispers to us that it is a waste of time, that that will not change anything, that we are what we are, and so on. And nevertheless, it is necessary. The circle revolves, the cycle returns to its point of departure. To forgo recommencing is to fall into stagnation, or to regress. Our vow of conversion of life expresses the need to keep on relaunching ourselves, to begin again every morning as if it were the first morning of our conversion, the first day of our monastic life. 'Morning by morning [the Lord] wakens – wakens my ear', says the Servant of the Lord, 'to listen as those who are taught' (Isaiah 50:4). Give us this day our daily bread. Morning and evening, beginning and end. Each day, all our life, is to be lived in that space that opens on to eternity.

Everything is possible, since Christ has come. In coming into this world, he brought total newness, the Fathers used to say. 'I am making all things new' (Revelation 21:5), as at the dawn of creation – because it is a question of a new creation.

> You have stripped off the old self with its practices and have clothed yourselves with the new self, which is being renewed in knowledge according to the image of its creator. In that renewal there is no longer Greek and Jew, circumcised and uncircumcised, barbarian, Scythian, slave and free; but Christ is all and in all! (Colossians 3:9b–11)

CREATION

The absolute beginning belongs to God alone. It is the creation, the being which springs up *ex nihilo*, out of nothing. It is already a message of hope.

> In the beginning when God created the heavens and the earth, the earth was a formless void and darkness covered the face of the deep, while a wind from God swept over the face of the waters. Then God said, 'Let there be light'; and there was light. And God saw that the light was good; and God separated the light from the darkness . . .
> Then God said, 'Let us make humankind in our image, according to our likeness . . .

> So God created humankind in his image,
>   in the image of God he created them;
> male and female he created them.
> (Genesis 1:1–3a, 26–27)

We have the assurance that at the source of all being and of all history is the creative goodness of God which pours out on to his creatures. The breath, the Spirit of God, hovers over the chaos, brings it under control and forms it according to God's plan. This creative action of God is not to be situated in a distant past, according to the perspective of science which seeks to know if, and when, the universe began. The assertion of Genesis is a theological assertion. It affirms God as the absolute source of being, and created being as hanging from the creative action of God, in a dependence as actual at this moment as a billion years ago. Creation springs up at each instant from God's hand. God infuses into us the being that we are, here and now. All our vital activity is produced by the divine vitality.

RE-CREATION

God himself follows the law of new beginnings. He must take the work of creation in hand once again, to complete it by a new creation. Not by an unforeseen, fortuitous addition – divine wisdom encompasses all things, sovereignly governs the time of history. The redemptive work of Christ only reveals another level of the depth of God's plan, hidden in the work of the first creation. Because:

> In the beginning was the Word, and the Word was with God, and the Word was God. (John 1:1)

> All things have been created through him and for him . . . he is the beginning. (Colossians 1:16, 18)

> 'I am the Alpha and the Omega, the first and the last, the beginning and the End.' (Revelation 22:13)

We were created in the image of God, that is to say, in the image of Christ, the exact imprint of God's very being (Hebrews 1:3). The second creation is the restoration of that image which sin disfigured, by the conformity of our being to that of Christ.

> And all of us, with unveiled faces, seeing the glory of the Lord as though reflected in a mirror, are being transformed into the same image from one degree of glory to another; for this comes from the Lord, the Spirit. (2 Corinthians 3:18)

The Spirit which hovered over the primitive chaos, hovers over the chaos of the obscure depths of our being, over the forces of division and violence; it unifies us and forms in us the image of God, in love, justice and truth.

> The true light, which enlightens everyone, was coming into the world.
>
> He was in the world, and the world came into being through him; yet the world did not know him. He came to what was his own, and his own people did not accept him. But to all who received him, who believed in his name, he gave power to become children of God, who were born, not of blood or of the will of the flesh or of the will of man, but of God. (John 1:9–13)

And we know well that Mary, the mother of Jesus and our mother, is there at this birth.

There is our hope and our task. It is the creative power of God that is working in us. It can realise everything in us, beyond our expectations. And we know with St Paul that 'the one who began a good work among you will bring it to completion by the day of Jesus Christ' (Philippians 1:6).

BEGINNINGS THAT NEVER HAVE AN END

Beyond the Parousia itself, I would dare to say, the law of beginnings extends to the eternity of God. The rhythm of new beginnings that marks our earthly life is the image of a rhythm of new beginnings in heaven.

Of the fullness of the incarnate Word, he who is in the bosom of the Father, and who reveals him to us, of this fullness we have, all of us, received – yes, 'grace upon grace' (John 1:16). The life of heaven is a participation in the divine knowledge and love. It is not something static, because God is infinite. To know him is to love him more. To love him more is to enter more deeply into his knowledge and thus, endlessly, for all eternity, into a communion which continually grows deeper.

Gregory of Nyssa is the great teacher of this doctrine:

> The pure heart sees God, according to the truthful word of our Master; but it receives him, in spiritual knowledge, in proportion to its capacity and according to its power. The incomprehensible infinity of the Deity dwells always beyond all capture. The greatness of the divine glory is

limitless, as the prophet affirms (Psalm 145:3): God remains what he is, in an ever equal transcendence . . . For the souls that ascend, the limit they have just discovered becomes the starting-point for a new and higher discovery. He who ascends does not cease to go from beginning to beginning, by beginnings that always surpass each other and never end. Desire never stops at what it knows; the soul passes continually from one desire to another greater desire; it pursues its path towards the infinite by ever-increasing ascents. (*On the Canticle* 44.941)

PILGRIMS

We are aliens and exiles on this earth (1 Peter 2:11), pilgrims on that ascent towards the holy city whose stages are celebrated by the psalms we recite each day at the little hours of the Office.

I was glad when they said to me:
'Let us go to the house of the Lord.'

(Psalm 122:1)

To you I lift up my eyes,
O you who are enthroned in the heavens!

(Psalm 123:1)

Happy is everyone who fears the Lord,
who walks in his ways.

(Psalm 128:1)

The Lord is so patient! A hundred times we take a wrong road, we draw back, we fall. A hundred times his pardon is renewed, his grace lifts us up again, his love rejoices at our return. That is the advantage we have over the angels: their whole being passes into their only act which fixes them eternally with regard to God; we, as long as this life lasts, can ceaselessly lift ourselves up again, ceaselessly recommence. And always the mercy of the Lord comes to meet us.

The steadfast love of the Lord never ceases,
his mercies never come to an end;

they are new every morning;
   great is your faithfulness.
'The Lord is my portion,' says my soul,
   'therefore I will hope in him.'

(Lamentations 3:22–24)

FORGETTING THE ROAD TRAVELLED AND STRAINING AHEAD . . .

On this road St Paul gives us a precious piece of advice. He threw himself with total ardour after Christ. All those privileges of the Jewish race and religion 'I came to regard as loss because of Christ . . . I want to know him and the power of his resurrection and the sharing of his sufferings . . . if somehow I may attain the resurrection from the dead.' (It is the new life St John speaks of.)

However, Paul does not believe that everything is done, that he can rest on his 'attainments', that he is perfect. Far from it!

> Not that I have already obtained this or have already reached the goal; but I press on to make it my own, because Christ Jesus has made me his own. Beloved, I do not consider that I have made it my own; but this one thing I do: forgetting what lies behind and straining forward to what lies ahead, I press on towards the goal for the prize of the heavenly call of God in Christ Jesus. (Philippians 3:12–14)

'Forgetting what lies behind'. Not only his sins, but all that he has done and suffered for God. Most often it is our riches that weigh us down. We are too weak not to appropriate them. We lose the blessedness of the poor for rubbish. Rather let us thank God for our poverty, even for our faults. Poverty is not an obstacle to God, our self-complacency is. Let us desire only the way of faith, of humility, of concrete, real, daily love. The past should be returned into the hands of the mercy of the Lord. Let us not lose time. Let us live intensely the present moment, the only real one, in its profound reality of movement towards the Father, like the eternal Word (John 1:1). Straining ahead, let us race for the finish, in response to the call from above which God addresses to us in Jesus Christ. 'Arise, my love, my fair one, and come away' (Song of Solomon 2:10).

> But our citizenship is in heaven, and it is from there that we are expecting a Saviour, the Lord Jesus Christ. He will transform the body of our humiliation so that it may be conformed to the body of his glory, by the power that also enables him to make all things subject to himself.
>
> (Philippians 3:20–21)

Come, Lord Jesus!

LENT

8

Awakening Life

The external rhythm of our life is determined by the movement of the liturgical year, itself in harmony with the movement of the seasons. They succeed each other in an ample life-cycle: birth, growth, maturity, decline, death. Each day is its micro-image. We are lucky that the harsh climate of our mountains* and the absence of many modern facilities that tend to neutralise the effects of the seasons, profoundly mark our life and make us sensitive to the rhythms of the cosmos.

At the moment we are in the grip of a harsh winter, of snow and ice. Life is dormant, the trees stripped of their foliage, it is piercing cold. Nevertheless, one senses a hidden hope of life which needs only a brief visit of the sun to manifest itself in the joyful song of the little birds that one believed to be gone elsewhere, and in the tumultuous gaiety of the streams swollen by the melting snow. Spring is coming! Life is awakening!

The Liturgy too has put on its sombre vestments, has stripped itself of its Alleluias and Gloria in Excelsis. It invites us to a certain narrowing of life, to a voluntary deprivation of what is superfluous, to a period of hidden and profound germination, illuminated always by a hope and an expectation. It invites us to return within ourselves in order to plunge once more into the sources of our life, that is to say, into Christ. It urges us to rediscover our true countenance in an effort of authenticity and lucidity, in prayer and charity, so that, modelled upon Christ, we may be capable of a deeper communion in his mystery.

For the mystery of Christ is not something outside us, it is what we are and what we are called to be. His drama is ours.

---

* The surroundings of the Grande Chartreuse.

Our cross is none other than that of Christ, it is his love in us that carries it. Our true life is the life of the Risen One in us. If the Liturgy leads us in the footsteps of Christ, it is in order to teach us the path that is also ours.

The drama to be found there evokes not only the recollection of a past event, but the actualisation of the drama of Christ, here and now, for us, placing before us the decisive option of faith and love, and the victorious power of his life and his love is communicated to us in the sacramental celebration of his mystery. That is clear in the sacrifice of the Mass and in the sacraments, where the Word of Christ, in and through the Church, realises what it announces (it is the Word of God) and signifies, in the symbols, acts and words. But that is also true of the liturgical cycle taken globally, though perhaps in a less intense manner, because it depends more on our subjective dispositions, but contains nevertheless a formative power which can be a considerable support in our effort to conform ourselves to Christ and to live in his Body, the Church.

So let us try to place ourselves in harmony with the spirit of the Liturgy of this time and to welcome the sap of life of which it is the bearer; according to the well-known expression of Pius XI, the Liturgy is the principal source of the Christian spirit.

ASH WEDNESDAY

> You are dust,
>   and to dust you shall return.
>
> (Genesis 3:19)

When? Tomorrow? Next year? In twenty years' time? It doesn't matter! This grain of dust on your forehead is your inescapable destiny. So employ your short years well, be converted, turn towards Christ who alone can give you pardon and life.

Thus we begin Lent, a time of conversion and austerity, but also a time of restrained joy, 'the joy of a purified heart' (the second Preface of Lent). It is a question of 'preparing oneself for the Paschal feast'. We are going to a feast!

'And whenever you fast, do not look dismal, like the hypocrites, for they disfigure their faces so as to show others
that they are fasting. Truly I tell you, they have received
their reward.' (Matthew 6:16)

So listen well to the Lord and take what he says as a norm
of conduct, not only for Lent, but for your whole life as a
monk, because the life of a monk is but one long preparation
for the definitive Paschal feast.

'But when you fast, put oil on your head and wash your
face, so that your fasting may be seen not by others but
by your Father who is in secret; and your Father who sees
in secret will reward you.' (Matthew 6:17–18)

The demands of these words, applied to all the deprivations
that we embrace or that we undergo, go a very long way.

During this week, at Matins, we sing the response about
Abraham, we meditate on his trial, the sacrifice of Isaac. 'Put
oil on your head and wash your face.' Your Father says so.
What grandeur there is at times in silence – not the silence of
transgression, but the silence of virtue that is perfect when it is
not even aware of itself – and what strength can be drawn
from it. Christian cheerfulness is the simplicity of faith, the
seriousness of hope, the vitality of love.

FROM ASH WEDNESDAY TO THE FIRST SUNDAY
OF LENT

These days specify again the spirit of the Christian fast: the
spirit of the Beatitudes, the spirit of poverty, humility and love.
'Beware of practising your piety before others.' 'Whenever you
pray, do not be like the hypocrites', who love to be seen by
others. 'But whenever you pray, go into your room and shut
the door and pray to your Father who is in secret; and your
Father who sees in secret will reward you' (Matthew 6:6).

As men of prayer, that therefore is our programme for Lent:
to go into that secret place, hidden from others, where only the
Father sees. We are called to an effort of recollection and

deepening. A hidden, solitary effort that no one else can accomplish for us. We must detach ourselves from all our petty preoccupations and attachments of self-love, and find the time to enter into the depths of our heart, in an effort of openness and lucidity, and pray to our Father there.

That demands perseverance and sometimes courage. For we must accept to be what we are with all our poverty. In that silence we must face up to our secret pains from which we try to flee by our activities and chatter. We must endure the obscurity of faith, because this secret place is hidden for us also – we do not see the Father. We have to lean on the Word of the Lord: 'Your Father knows what you need, before you ask him.' My Father knows! What a reassurance one gets in the embrace of his love to which one must surrender all in secret, in the darkness, sometimes in suffering! He knows. He understands.

Let us try to allow the prayer of Christ, the prayer of the Son, to well up in us. Our prayer is not a question of technique, of tricks, of subjective emotions, however sublime, of knowledge, however deep. It is something infinitely greater than us; it extends far and wide beyond the capacities of our heart. It is the prayer of Christ in us: a prayer that has its source in the eternal love of the Son for the Father, receiving everything from him, returning everything to him, in a perfect gift of self. It is a prayer-love which expresses itself in the human language of the 'Abba' on the lips of Christ, in his nights of solitary contemplation on the mountain, in his whole life and charity, above all in his death 'for us' on the wood of the Cross. He gave us his Spirit, put his love in our hearts, the source of his prayer in us. He is 'Abba', 'Father' – source of that charity towards our brothers which the prophets defined as 'the fast that God prefers' (Isaiah 58:1–9). Prayer-love which embraces all our brothers, all people of all times. May this prayer-love which transcends time and space dwell in us for our few moments of existence and then these moments will be, in some way, eternal.

The first reading of Saturday's Mass, Philippians 3:8–14, sums up the essence of our Lent.

I want to know Christ and the power of his resurrection
and the sharing of his sufferings by becoming like him in
his death, if somehow I may attain the resurrection from
the dead. (Philippians 3:10–11)

So St Paul says, in the awareness of having been 'made his
own' by Christ. Paul has only one care:

Forgetting what lies behind and straining forward to what
lies ahead, I press on towards the goal for the prize of the
heavenly call of God in Christ Jesus. (Philippians 3:13–14)

Our preparation in expectation of Easter should be borne along
by a similar impetus.

9

With Christ in the Desert

Our 'fast', we have seen, consists only in removing the obstacles to our profound conformation to Christ. We cannot take any other model but him. So the Liturgy reads the account of the temptation of Christ in the desert (Matthew 4:1–11) on the first Sunday of Lent.

Our Statutes propose this mystery to us with a certain insistence: 'According to the monastic tradition, it is up to us to follow Christ in his fast in the desert, treating the body severely and reducing it to servitude, so that the desire for God will enlighten the spirit' (Statutes 16.1).

What is the meaning of this episode in the life of Christ? – because it has a meaning for him; it was not play-acting but a very real test. At the Jordan, Christ has just been anointed with the Spirit and referred to as 'beloved Son', in view of his mission of redemption. Then he is 'led up by the Spirit into the wilderness to be tempted by the devil' (Matthew 4:1). What temptation? To use his relationship to God ('if you are the Son of God'), and so to use God, in order to have bread (and every earthly commodity); to mesmerise the crowds by an ostentatious miracle; to submit to Satan in order to dominate the world politically.

For Jesus, it is a question of choosing the way to accomplish his messianic mission, to confirm the role of Suffering Servant already hinted at at the Baptism ('my Beloved' – cf. Isaiah 42:1), to leave aside the human and even the supernatural means at his disposal. He sets out the principles that would guide his whole mission and lead him to the Cross: absolute obedience to the will of God ('to live on every word that comes from the mouth of God'); trust in God without demanding proof ('do not put the Lord your God to the test'); and an allegiance to God which takes precedence over every other ('worship the Lord your God, and serve only him').

The whole drama of the life of Christ is already here. It is through a mission that ends in apparent failure that the humble servant must announce the Good News to the poor. That drama is always repeated in the desert: the choice of spiritual means, so humanly poor; a trust and a faith great enough to do without proofs even when God seems entirely absent; and rejection of every idol, including that idol so dear to us, our own ego, to adore God alone.

Like Christ we must take the sword of the Word of God to defend ourselves against the attacks of the devils and the weaknesses and complacencies of our spirit. 'Teach us to always hunger for Christ, the only living and true bread, and to live from every word that comes from his mouth' (Post-Communion Prayer).

In the person of Christ it is the new People of God who overcome in the trial. The drama has an ecclesial dimension. It is the same with our own: it is the faith of the entire Church that struggles in the soul of the solitary.

The first reading of the Mass (2 Corinthians 6:1–10) strikes a note of urgency, orchestrated by the first two responses of Matins: 'Now is the acceptable time; see, now is the day of salvation!' (6:2a). One must never reduce the Liturgy to a meditation on the past. It is rather the irruption of a reality which transcends time and space and which bursts in on me at this moment in time, at this point in space. The temptation of Christ presents itself to me as a choice to be made here and now; and because Christ has triumphed, he makes that choice and that faith possible in me.

There is a grace in this Lent for you and me, a grace quite individual, which is, besides, linked in some way to this moment, and which will never more return. 'There is a tide in the affairs of men' (Shakespeare) – and of God.

The formulary of the Mass is composed largely of verses from Psalm 91, that great cry of trust in the protection of God, which Satan wished to turn into presumption. The Word of

God invites us to that trust, but at the same time does not hide the demands of God.

> 'From there you will seek the Lord your God, and you will find him if you search after him with all your heart and soul . . . Because the Lord your God is a merciful God.' (Deuteronomy 4:29, 31a)

10

Isaac Recovered

The story of the temptation of Abraham (Genesis 22:1–19) is not 'edifying' in the ordinary sense of the term. It is frightening, disturbing. One could not propose it lightly for imitation by everyone in general. Our Lord taught us rather to pray: 'Lead us not into temptation'. Let no one overestimate his strength. Such a trial is only bearable if God takes the initiative in it and gives the strength to bear it. In fact, who is he who knows with certainty that he believes? And Isaac is returned only to him who does not doubt. There lies the real paradox in all that: that Isaac is recovered. Too easily, we identify the courage of faith with the courage of renunciation. Certainly, one cannot do without renunciation. Only he who lifted the knife receives Isaac. But the courage of faith goes further.

Faith begins by surrendering oneself totally to God; that is absolutely necessary. But that God is a God who promises, and the eyes of faith are turned towards the fulfilment of the promise. Isaac is born. So faith finds, on the human level, a concrete realisation; this points from afar to the full realisation, that numerous race that is to be born; but the first link is already given: faith possesses a human support.

Now, by fidelity to this God in whom he believes, Abraham gets ready to sacrifice Isaac, who seemed to be the humanly indispensable means of fulfilling the promise; and nevertheless, Abraham continues to adhere, in faith and hope, to the totality of the word of God: so he still believes in the promise, never revoked by God. Thus, at this moment, his faith has no longer any other support except a trust in God, 'eyes closed', despite the humanly evident impossibility of seeing the promise accomplished. It is then, and then only, that he receives anew the fruit of that promise – but with hands that know themselves to be totally empty – as a pure gift of God's grace, a gift that is totally transparent to the love of the Giver. From now on, divine love can freely invade and inundate with its riches the man who has become totally poor, pure receptivity; Abraham does not appropriate the gift, and does not become proud because of it. But note well, the positive orientation of faith, and the thirst for life, love and being that drive him on were true, and were fulfilled beyond measure, paradoxically but truly, and to a certain extent already in this life. Isaac is recovered. All the same, something in the relationship of Abraham with God and of Abraham with his son can never again be as it was before.

Monastic life sometimes entails something analogous. The beginner in religious life gives up everything to follow Christ. But he is like a man who penetrates for the first time into the desert. He cuts off the human supports of his life, he rejects the precious waters of liberty, of human love and so on, with great generosity, but with a courage sustained by the presumption of inexperience. Lofty ideals seem as if within reach and he sees himself surrounded by a sort of glorious aura. Little by little the gift of himself in faith takes root in monastic life; it is structured by it, it receives a visible form, at the same time expression and support. That is absolutely necessary for him so that the delicate germ of his vocation can grow. His intellect becomes intoxicated with the light that the contemplation of divine revelation brings him; his will is strengthened by the order and harmony of a life in which every step has a meaning; his sensibility is charmed by the austere beauty of the chant; his heart is comforted by the presence of brothers walking by his side on the same path. He has written his promise on a parchment; it is accepted by the Church. The Kingdom of God begins to be realised already – visibly. All that is good; it is the fruit of his faith, of his prayer; it is the fulfilment of the promise; it is the divine blessing; it is Isaac. He must use the human means that God puts within his reach; to neglect them would be the presumption that 'tempts God'. But the kind of security that these means give him, the light and the warmth that they bring, could also make them shield him from an infinitely more subtle light and heat, situated beyond human grasp, from an absence of support infinitely stronger than the petty justice within human capabilities which he industriously seeks to build and behind which he is always in danger of installing himself, sheltered from the excessively exacting demands of this God who does not know moderation. One is so much at home in the midst of things, ideas, rules and ceremonies; one is a master at it! One pays the tithe of adoration to God, but one is careful to leave hermetically sealed all the doors that could let God himself enter.

But the years pass and, before the eyes of the monk, the horizon unceasingly recedes. He learns the value of the water, formerly forsaken so lightheartedly, by the crucifying effects of thirst. He looks on, helplessly, as his body wilts and loses its vigour, while he is overcome with weariness. He seems to forget where he is going and why. What use is a heart so dried up that it seems incapable of loving others and consequently God himself (for we have only one heart for loving)? Is it that the 'means' destroyed the 'end'? Progressively – or in a sudden crisis – the meaning of his life will be called into question.

Or perhaps he will stumble by a fountain of earthly water, pure and fresh, in some hidden oasis. A very great moral effort is then necessary to renounce the satisfaction of that thirst which is at the very root of his soul: an effort incomparably greater and more painful than his initial renunciation.

The monk is humble now and without illusions. The sand of life that he holds in his hand flows rapidly through his fingers; his eyes have difficulty in seeing beyond the limits of human horizons, he knows his indigence, his human weakness, his human heart. He is not sure that he continues to believe in what he cannot see. Rites and ceremonies say very little to him, the repetition of acts that do not correspond to an interior spontaneity tends to produce a certain 'alienation' of his personality. The well-organised structures of his life hem him in like the bars of a prison where everything seems sterile and dead. He only touches his brothers exteriorly, in passing; he feels alone, alien.

The fact is that God is in the process of taking Isaac back, and the monk must freely surrender that which seemed to be the humanly indispensable means for the fulfilment of the promise of the Kingdom of God, or what appeared to be that Kingdom – and that without doubting, without forsaking that quest for the absolute, for Love, which now seems to be null and void, illusory; one must cling in faith and hope to the Word of God and to the promise of Christ, to the power of the Spirit of Christ to give life to what seems to be dead, without faith having any other support but a 'blind' trust in God alone. That is the specific courage of faith, the courage to believe that one receives, and to receive in fact, already, everything, absolutely everything from the pure gratuitousness of God's love.

The situation is no longer the same as at the beginning. There is not now a choice between different ways of living which open up before the beginner, equally full of promise. Life is a one-way street: there is no means of turning back. The tested man has no illusion about the possibility of fully realising himself, of satisfying the deep desires of his heart, on a purely human level. He knows himself to be made for God; he is too marked now. The choice that presents itself to him is a choice between a life which has a transcendent meaning (though perceived solely in the obscurity of faith), and a life in which that meaning would be relegated in fact to a very distant secondary plane, a life where he would satisfy himself with a water within his reach, within his capabilities. We must not deceive ourselves about the real possibility of such a choice; how many, among the people of our time, opt for the obscure wait? When one thirsts in real earnest, a cup of water has a force of immense attraction. That is what we are like.

Once again one must abandon all into the Lord's hands, but an 'all' measured more justly and loved more deeply; and that, not with bitterness or despair, but in the confidence of the faith that in Christ one possesses all, even in the present. 'Truly I tell you, there is no one who has left [everything] for the sake of the kingdom of God, who will not get back very much more *in this age*, and in the age to come eternal life' (Luke 18:29–30). This movement should be real, should be total; but if it is, it is possible that 'Isaac' will be given to us in God, even in this life: light, brothers, the positive meaning of the institution – all could be recovered; but it is perhaps in the sphere of interpersonal relationships, from now on 'in Christ', that the greatest deepening is possible. Yet it will be a gift consecrated to God by the gesture of sacrifice, under the sign of Christ, and in a manner *within* Christ: an 'Isaac' who, in Christ, is pure joy, and who, one knows however, will be fully given only in the fullness of Christ, but then for all eternity; an 'Isaac' possessed in hope.

The monk, the Christian, is necessarily a person of hope whose whole being strives in faith towards the true water of eternal life and love, and who, all along the way, is sustained by that water as by an interior, hidden source.

Come, Lord Jesus!

11

Transfiguration

In our Carthusian Liturgy, on this Sunday the Gospel of the previous Thursday (the Syrophoenician woman) was repeated. In the recent renewal, Sunday's Gospel became that of the Transfiguration (Matthew 17:1–9) formerly read on the Saturday preceding it. These great Gospels of the first two Sundays of Lent, the Temptation and the Transfiguration, by their contrast give its style to Lent: shadow and light, the struggle against evil, and divine enlightenment. The whole contrast of Lent places the mystery of the Transfiguration in a different light from that given it in the feast of the Transfiguration. The theme of Lent puts forward the relationship with the Baptism and temptation on the one hand and the death and the Resurrection of Christ on the other. The Liturgy is a constant to-and-fro between the themes of death and resurrection, because it is always the efficacious presence of the Risen Christ in his whole mystery.

There is a close connection between the temptation and the Transfiguration of Christ. We have seen that the temptation is the sequel of the Baptism and anointing of Christ. The symmetry of language in the Baptism and the Transfiguration is striking: the voice of the Father repeats once more the same expression: 'This is my Son, the Beloved; with him I am well pleased', and he adds with a new degree of insistence: 'Listen to him!' But there is a distinct progress in the revelation of God's plan. Here it becomes clear that the mission of Jesus, Servant of the Lord, can only be realised by his death. It was about his 'exodus' (his death) which he was going to accomplish in Jerusalem, that he was speaking with Moses and Elijah (Luke 9:31). And, if God gives the disciples a glimpse of the mysterious glory of his Son, it is to fortify them against the scandal of his death, by showing them in anticipation something of the glory of his resurrection.

The temptation took place in the desert; the revelation of Jesus' glory took place on a high mountain where he took three of his favourite disciples aside to pray. There they saw him as he really was, he the beloved Son of the Father. There they were prepared to participate in his Paschal mystery.

To illustrate the profound roots of this event in the plan of God, as a first reading we have the account of the ascent of Moses on Mt Sinai where he remained for forty days and forty nights. The glory of the Lord appeared in the form of a devouring fire (Exodus 24:12–18). On the mountain of the Transfiguration, the glory of the Lord radiates on the face of Christ (2 Corinthians 4:6). Human beings always feel a reverence mingled with fear ('awe') before the divine revelation. The disciples fall to the ground face down, conscious of their nothingness. But when they look again, there is no longer anyone, but Jesus only. He comes close, touches them and says: 'Stand up! Do not be afraid.'

There is no longer a cloud, no longer a voice from heaven, no longer a brilliant light. There is no longer anyone but Jesus only. A man by all appearances, like others. A man who is going to die, for us. For an instant you have seen the divine dimension of his human reality. Until the Resurrection you must be content to walk in faith. God with you, it will be Jesus only. Is it that God was so close to us, so 'evident' that we did not see him? We sought something new, spectacular. But all the time the light was hidden in the banal reality before our eyes. All that is light for him who has eyes to see. Jesus only. The man only in all his weakness and hidden greatness. Human life, human realities, human love and death, the cosmos. Don't look for anything else. 'Stand up!' Head high, walk along your path with courage and confidence. 'Do not be afraid!'

Go beyond that fear you have of God. A fear good in its time, part of the divine pedagogy. But now you must go much further and embrace God in Jesus, in this man, your brother. You must not be afraid. The love of God, so close to us in

Jesus, is too great. Let us open our heart rather, taking a risk on God in Christ, becoming sons in him, men with him.

> And all of us, with unveiled faces, seeing the glory of the Lord as though reflected in a mirror, are being transformed into the same image from one degree of glory to another; for this comes from the Lord, the Spirit. (2 Corinthians 3:18)

One of the Scripture readings of the week describes this process in the following way:

> You were taught to put away your former way of life . . . and to be renewed in the spirit of your mind, and to clothe yourselves with the new self, created according to the likeness of God in true righteousness and holiness. (Ephesians 4:22a, 23–24)

– an interior transformation brought about by God through the force of the truth, resulting in sanctity, that is to say, conformity to Christ.

12

The Samaritan Woman

The third and fourth weeks of Lent have in common the fact of being more centred on the theme of Baptism. Historically, they were conceived as the important time of preparation of the catechumens. The ancient Masses of pre-baptismal scrutinies are to be found in them, and many formularies develop the themes of new birth, light, living water and so on. The Roman liturgy has in recent years restored the great baptismal Gospels to the third, fourth and fifth Sundays of Lent, though the Carthusian liturgy, for practical reasons, retains them on certain weekdays of the third and fourth weeks.

Above all, the Liturgy invites us during these weeks to deepen the meaning of our Baptism and to revive in ourselves the grace of our insertion into Christ. That is full of meaning in the context of Lent, for to be converted, for us, never consists in a merely moral and ascetic effort which could remain on a human level. Our Christian being comes from somewhere else, and to revive it is to immerse ourselves once more in the source from which it flows.

THE OFFER OF TRUE LIFE

We are all like the Samaritan woman in Friday's Gospel (John 4:5–42). The Lord offers us true life, the gift of the Spirit, which will become in us 'a spring of water gushing up to eternal life'. We are happy to receive this sublime gift, but we have great difficulty in remaining at that height. We trivialise it, we degrade it, we reduce it to our measure, an object to possess among others, merits to accumulate, an insurance against death, a fetish against the fear of life, an excuse for our incapacity to love. We surround it with all kinds of defences like a fragile plant: cultural and moral prohibitions, all sorts of exclusive rights.

But that is not the living water that Christ gives. On the contrary, it is a dynamic force of love, the Spirit of love (John 7:39), which shatters all the limits, all the divisions (4:21). It matters little if it is on the mountain of Samaria or that of Jerusalem that one worships, provided one worships in spirit and in truth, that is to say, in the love poured into our hearts by the Holy Spirit and in the truth brought by Christ. St Paul will say 'Where the Spirit of the Lord is, there is freedom' (2 Corinthians 3:17). And St John repeats untiringly that it is by the love we have, for God and for the neighbour, that 'we know that we abide in God and he in us because he has given us of his Spirit' (1 John 4:13).

The gift we have received is a flowing spring that carries us (and not we that carry it!), that vivifies us, makes us capable of loving in truth, in Christ; it is the source of worship of the Father. Meditate on that extraordinary phrase: 'The Father seeks' these worshippers. The Father seeks us, because we want to adore him in truth and we seek the Father. That is the drama of our life. And it is possible that it is to the indifferent and unworthy sinner in us that the Lord who does not observe the conventions will offer the living water. There is a continuity between the water of the well and eternal water. Love, to the extent that it is true, is always identical to itself, always eternal. It is traditional to apply the image of living water to the grace of contemplation (see, for example, St Teresa of Avila), the effort of drawing water from the well to meditation. That falls within the perspective of our programme of deepening our life of prayer during this Lent, without, for all that, separating that from a deepening of the life of Christ in us, of the ascendancy of the Spirit over our heart. The result should be the welling up in us of that adoration which is one of the highest fruits of love, of the Spirit in us, and which can only lead us in the truth of a silence full of praise, and of a solitude charged with communion. But I am afraid of being caught in the snare of words here. 'To adore in spirit and in truth.' We all desire it, or at least we think we desire it. The truth is a burning flame and the Spirit eludes our control and leads us where we do not wish to go.

It was so simple at the beginning! To adore, that was to express a homage full of respect, veneration and obedience, by solemn chants, solemn prayers, hieratic gestures, by moral conduct according to well-determined rules, by silent, interior prayers, finally, by a love full of gratitude. One was not wicked, one was sure of this God and a little self-satisfied.

So, one after another, the elements of this solidly constructed world have collapsed. They all depended on a certain idea of God, and this idea has vanished, as it were. One speaks a great deal of the death of God nowadays, often in an unacceptable way. But you will permit me the risk of saying that for each of us there is a moment when God must die. In one sense, only the atheist (*a-theos*, without-God) can truly believe in God. Let me explain: it is necessary that the God of our imagination, the God of our projections and desires (who is none other than our Ego deified) die; the God who stands alongside the cosmos as some 'thing' else, who stands alongside the neighbour as someone else, in competition with him to win my love; the God of whom it suffices to know the general moral rules to do his will; the God infinitely above creatures' pains in a transcendence beyond reach; the God-judge, who punishes through the demands of a justice conceived according to our human standards; the God who cramps the spontaneity of life and love. That one must die, to make room for a God strangely close and familiar and nevertheless totally elusive. Who bears a human face, that of Christ, that of my brother. Who is love in a way that defies all our human notions of justice. Who is generosity, overflowing life, gratuitousness, unpredictable liberty. Who does nothing 'in general', but who is always 'You' facing 'me'. Supreme personality in the total gift of himself, he is in the inmost depths of every person, the source of every personality, never alongside human persons (but distinct from them); in loving them, I share in his love and I love himself. He is not to be thought of in opposition to created reality (because he is not a thing), he reveals himself through its contours, its limits and its beauty; however, he is not created

reality, he is of a different order. He is neither presence nor
absence for my senses and intelligence. He is neither more
nor less. His true greatness is his humility which impelled him
to become man. His wealth is the poverty of love. He has
suffered – eternally? – while being infinite Bliss.

I speak of him, so do I know him? By my experience I do
not know him. I have not found him among created beings, I
have not seen his trace in the events of my life, I have not found
him within me – everything there is created, human, everything
has its explanation at this level. I cannot express him with my
words. So there only remains for me the face of Christ, the
human and the created, and his Word in Sacred Scripture and
in the Church (note it well, this Word always comes to me
through the intermediary of others). Am I finally in the 'truth'?
Have I found in not finding?

How should I adore him if this is what he is like?

I said that only the atheist can truly believe in God, for only
the atheist has nothing else but the human. So he has the
possibility of letting his whole being, if he assumes it fully and
lucidly, go into an act of faith and of gift of himself which
opens on to the pure Mystery of a God who is All and Nothing.
It is not only the God adored who has vanished, as we used to
say: the adorer also has collapsed under the demoralising effect
of a more and more profound lucidity concerning the complex
ambiguities of his actions. Little by little, the hidden layers of
the psyche are laid bare, the evasions, the detours of egoism
and fear, the many wolves who present themselves as lambs,
the corruption of the heart, the very source of all our acts and
prayers. One recognises that the pious praying person of former
times was only a mask, at least in part; his veneration was an
instinctive fear before the invisible and the judge; his obedience
a calculation and a constraint; his love a subjective emotion
produced quite artificially and out of proportion to his meagre
accomplishments in concrete life; his austerity, the expression
of a masochistic desire for self-punishment in order to allay a
neurotic guilt-complex; his desire for solitude, the evasion of
an incomplete personality who does not know how to join in
the life of human beings.

One could continue indefinitely. All that is clearly exaggerated and, nevertheless, partly true. For every virtue has its shadow and is never realised in a pure state. Every authentic movement of the soul has a counterfeit and we are located, nearly always, somewhere between the two extremes. All our human acts are ambiguous.

How should I adore if this is what I am like?

To pray in spirit and in truth implies that we accept ourselves in total lucidity just as we are. Not passively, crushed by the weight of a fate from which there is no escape, but with courage and energy, turning our good qualities to the best account while forestalling the incursions of our bad qualities. We have received the energy of the Spirit of Christ. We will not lose courage for, in the last analysis, we will not count on a justice of our own but on Christ, in faith. He will give us, create out of nothing, the good works that will give him glory. It could be – and that applies especially, I believe, to the solitary – that our trust (in spite of our very real poverty), our desire to love (in spite of our feeble efficacy), our thirst, our hope, give him the most glory. His will is love. One has only to embrace it with filial devotion. That is in no way depressing or servile. On the contrary, it is a true liberation because our poverty, in itself, is not a boon. But to accept ourselves as we are, that is to situate ourselves in the truth; and over against this true self there is the love of God, which itself is infinitely rich. Our poverty is the measure of our receptivity, not only of God's gifts, but of God himself in the union of love. We should seek this poverty, as a pane of glass would seek to be perfectly transparent, so as to become purely light. In love, all is joy and liberty, like God himself. To pray in spirit and in truth, in purity of heart to seek God, in the spirit of the Beatitudes, is always a question of the same thing, and it is our entire life as monks.

> Wash yourselves; make yourselves clean;
>   remove the evil of your doings
>   from before my eyes;
> cease to do evil,
>   learn to do good . . .

Though your sins are like scarlet,
   they shall be like snow;
though they are red like crimson,
   they shall become like wool.

                              (Isaiah 1:16, 17a, 18b)

13

The Man Born Blind

The Liturgy, with more than one Father of the Church, sees in the cure of the man born blind (John 9:1–38), at the pool of Siloe (that is to say, of the Sent), the symbol of baptismal regeneration: to be immersed in the pool of the Sent one, is to be baptised in Christ (St Augustine), it is the ascent of humankind from natural darkness to the light of Christ.

The blind beggar is likeable, and the itinerary of his faith is rich in lessons on the conflict between light and darkness in the human soul. Let us pick out some of them, and I will leave the rest to your meditation.

First of all, let us note Christ's action smearing the blind man's eyes with a little mud mixed to a paste with his saliva. Why this act which only aggravates the blindness of the disabled man? Maybe he wanted to test his faith and oblige him to co-operate in his own healing by washing off the mud at the pool. Christ's gesture would then be an invitation to abandon himself to him, literally, eyes closed. We can agree with certain Fathers of the Church in seeing in it a figure of the Incarnation (Augustine, Bede). The humanity of Christ is the created instrument which brings us the light, but to see the divinity clearly, we are obliged to pass beyond, and that by the active co-operation of our act of faith.

All is not done in a moment. We see the blind man rising by degrees, through his rectitude and faithfulness, from the light that is given him at each stage, to an ever higher understanding both of the occurrence of which he is the beneficiary and of the person of Jesus, until he finally reaches faith. It is a continuous ascent from darkness to full daylight.

At the beginning, Jesus, for him, is only 'the man called Jesus', as much as to say a stranger, and the opening of his

closed eyes is an incomprehensible adventure; he only grasps
its external particulars. But the very arguments of the Pharisees
and their bad faith disclose its religious sense to him. This Jesus
is 'a prophet', 'a devout man' who 'accomplishes God's will',
who prays, whom God answers and whom he sent to cure him.
He will not be swayed from his opinion. The blind man has
reached that point when Jesus finds him again. Driven out
ignominiously by the Pharisees, the doctors of the law, he is on
the threshold of faith. In order to consent to it fully, he still
needs that encounter. Finding him receptive, Jesus reveals
himself to him as the 'Son of Man', that is to say, he who
comes from heaven to gather humankind and raise them to
participation in the life of God (John 1:51; 3:14–15; 6:62–63).
The blind man accepts without argument: 'Lord, I believe.' He
'sees' with his new eyes the one who made him see: that was
the true goal of the miracle. The beggar, the man born blind,
who was 'sin, nothing but sin, since his birth', becomes the
living sign of humankind enlightened by Christ, the witness of
faith in Jesus-Light.

The attitude of the Pharisees casts a harsh light on the progress of the light in the depths of the human heart. Human
beings are, at the same time, light and darkness. We bear within
ourselves the power to blind ourselves; to give ourselves good
reasons for not seeing, to create false evidence for ourselves, to
refuse to open our eyes, saying that we 'see'. The fact is that
the light is demanding. It obliges one to reappraise so many
things, to give up so many habits, to break sometimes with a
whole environment. Our eyes are disturbed by it. We must
recover the purity of childhood.

It is not the fact of being blind that is tragic. Only Jesus can
give the eyes of faith – no one can see by themselves. What is
tragic is that those who are blind claim to see clearly. They
rebel against all healing, because they do not want to see. Their
pride closes their eyes to every light.

'The eye is the lamp of the body. So, if your eye is healthy,
your whole body will be full of light; but if your eye is

unhealthy, your whole body will be full of darkness. If then the light in you is darkness, how great is the darkness!' (Matthew 6:22–23)

And what the eye is to the body, the heart is to actions.

That could happen to the Pharisees, but not to us, you say! Careful, it is not certain. A perfect receptivity to the light is rare. All the more so because we are always in danger of installing ourselves in the measure of light we have received up to now and to which we have given form and substance in our life, and of refusing to travel the road that remains ahead of us, that will always remain ahead of us. Our life is Paschal, we attain a new degree of life by dying to the degree that we possess, we never have the right to cry 'halt!' to this movement, whatever it may cost us. After all, the Pharisees quote Moses, who was an authentic messenger of God, as their authority, in order to refuse the light of Christ. The light they were clinging to came from God, but its hour had come; a greater light had appeared. They appropriated the partial light and were not yet receptive to the total light.

Progress in the light of faith is a more and more radical spoliation. The solitary life can give the appearance of an altogether static life, from which every element of real progress and risk is excluded. Mistake! In the course of its perfectly monotonous development, a route is travelled, full of unforeseen events and surprises, marked periodically by fundamental choices at an ever deeper level. It is an eminently risky life, no one goes through it unscathed.

For our part, let us try to follow the example of our friend, the man born blind, and to be faithful to the light that is in us here and now. God will do the rest. It is he who gives at the same time 'the will and the work' (cf. Philippians 2:12–13). It is he alone who can give us that purity of heart without which nothing has value.

He promised it. Rightly on this day we read the great prophecy of Ezekiel (36:23–28), which at one and the same time expresses our desire and pins our hopes on God. Note this repeated 'I': it is the Lord who speaks, who acts. Historically, the prophets arrived at the conviction (inspired by God) of the necessity of a new human creation by a direct intervention of God, starting with the experience they have of the radical incapacity of Israel, of humankind, to keep the law of God by itself. It is out of this darkness that there arose the light Christ announced and the new birth of Baptism.

> I will sprinkle clean water upon you, and you shall be clean from all your uncleannesses, and from all your idols I will cleanse you. A new heart I will give you, and a new spirit I will put within you; and I will remove from your body the heart of stone and give you a heart of flesh. I will put my spirit within you, and make you follow my statutes and be careful to observe my ordinances . . . And you shall be my people, and I will be your God. (Ezekiel 36:25–28)

It is our heart itself, the root of our actions and our love, the light that is in us, that is corrupted. The healing that God proposes is radical: to give us a new heart and a new spirit; instead of our heart of stone, a heart of flesh. That can only be the heart of Christ, the Word made flesh; a human heart, but bearer of a divine love. The Lord also promises to put his own Spirit within us. So, interiorly renewed, having in us the heart and Spirit of Christ, we will walk according to his will, we will be his and he ours.

> Heal me, O Lord, and I shall be healed;
>   save me, and I shall be saved;
>   for you are my praise.
>
> (Jeremiah 17:14)

14

Rejoice with Jerusalem!

'Rejoice with Jerusalem: be glad for her, all you who love her.'
The Church who prepares her catechumens with such care,
and who formerly, on this Sunday, gave them the Credo, the
rule of their faith, anticipates the joy of receiving them fully
into communion with her, by a lyrical chant, the Introit of the
Mass. But right in the middle of Lent? Yes! The joy of
the Resurrection is never far from the lips of the Church, for
it is always the song of the Risen Christ that she offers to the
Father.

The Gospel of this Sunday is the account of the multipli-
cation of the loaves, by St John (John 6:1–14), sign of the
Eucharist, clearly indicated as such in the discourse following
this Gospel, which we read on the previous Thursday (John
6:15–35).

Church, Eucharist and Baptism are intimately linked.

The sacrament of Baptism is not a private affair between me
and Christ. Certainly, for me it is a new birth – purifying and
sanctifying (John 3:5; Ezekiel 36:25f.) in the Spirit and in the
grace of Christ. But this birth is produced by my sacramental
insertion into the Church through which the divine-human
life of Christ the Saviour has already found a corporeal and
sacramental presence in the world. Insertion in the Church is
the first effect of Baptism and, at the same time, the means of
attaining the fullness of renewal and justification of the old self
(Ephesians 4:22; Colossians 1:10) in an interior divinisation
and an assimilation to the death and resurrection of Jesus Christ
(Romans 6) by the power of his Spirit present in the Church.

Those are the dogmatic facts, and formerly they were clearly
underscored in the plenary baptismal celebration, precisely that
of the Easter Vigil, for which the Liturgy of these days prepares

us. That celebration took place at the heart of the eucharistic celebration, sacrament par excellence of Christ's victory over sin and death. Baptism appeared clearly there as the act by which the Church, in one single action, receives new believers into the community of the faith and integrates them into the Mystical Body of Christ by welcoming them to the eucharistic table. Baptism, in fact, crowned by Confirmation, by conforming us to Christ in the mystery of his redemptive death, makes us members of a totally priestly people. By so doing it introduces us to the Eucharist, where his people share, in the unity of faith, by common prayer, the sacrificial offering and communion with the Risen One, in this unique sacrifice of reconciliation and thanksgiving of which Christ is the priest.

Our Baptism, our insertion into Christ, is realised by our insertion into the Church, the Body of Christ. Its goal is only reached in the completion of the risen Body of Christ by the full participation of all the elect in his eternal life. Our destiny as baptised persons opens onto the plenitude of the total Christ, of the whole Church. Our beatitude will only be complete in the beatitude of all the members. That ultimate goal is in some way already inaugurated in the Eucharist. There, the offering of all our lives is assumed and becomes the offering of Christ by Christ. There, the individual life of each one is plunged into Love, which will be our beatitude for all eternity, and which is already realised in the union of all of us who are united to the Risen Christ. The communion in his unique sacrifice is the communion of brothers among themselves, is the plenitude of Christ. The participation of all at the conventual Mass, communicating in the one bread and one chalice, is the visible, sacramental expression of the final reality of heaven. Let us try to become fully conscious of it and to live it in depth.

So, in our effort, this Lent, to deepen the grace of Baptism, let us not neglect our union with our brothers. Christ does not come to us alone. The sap of his life in us passes through the arteries of his Body, the Church. We are brothers in him. It cannot be otherwise: blood claims its due. Brotherhood demands love, acceptance, compassion, mutual aid. Not only by prayer, in an invisible way – a precious reality, but not the total reality. Our communion from its origin is sacramental, that is to say, an invisible reality expressed and carried by a visible reality. Our love and our brotherhood must also become incarnate.

There is an aspect of our brotherhood on which some gospels of this time insist: it is the forgiveness of the faults of others.

> Then Peter came and said to [Jesus], 'Lord, if another member of the church sins against me, how often should I forgive? As many as seven times?' Jesus said to him, 'Not seven times, but, I tell you, seventy-seven times.' (Matthew 18:21–22)

That is to say, indefinitely.

As God forgave us in Christ, that should be our measure. Let us avoid deceiving ourselves with all the good reasons we can find for not forgiving: zeal for the rule, example to others, etc. Let us remember Jesus' response to those who were accusing the adulterous woman in front of him: 'Let anyone among you who is without sin be the first to throw a stone at her' (John 8:7b).

Jesus does not condemn, he saves by his forgiveness and love.

15

Lazarus

The Liturgy, above all in the fourth week, lets the hope of Jesus' victory over evil and over death pierce through the sombre clouds of the threat which gradually takes shape before him. On Thursday and Friday, it recalls the resurrections worked by Elisha and Elijah, and those that have Jesus himself for author: the resurrection of the son of the widow of Nain, and above all Lazarus. The divine power will not only conquer the darkness in the human spirit, it will also defeat that mortality which is the law of the flesh, the final word, without reply, of all our aspirations. Death, we know, is born of sin. If Christ wants to save us, he cannot shy away from this last adversary, the most terrible of all.

But the resurrections of which we have just spoken are only respites, returns to this life, unhoped-for prolongations, if you like, but all they do is to postpone a little the fatal day of death. However, they show that the power of God has power over death. They give a support to the hope of an eschatological resurrection. But this belief is only attested in the last books of the Old Testament and it is far from being that of all the Jews, or from being perfectly clear. In fact, in the book of Wisdom, it seems to be rather an incursion of Greek philosophy and a consequence of the natural immortality of the soul, a doctrine which is not self-evident philosophically and which scarcely enters into the perspective of the books of the Pentateuch, the Prophets and the Psalms. Even for the Jews, above all of pharisaic tendency, who believed in the general resurrection, this belief had the air of a challenge to the definitive triumph of evil, a piercing appeal to the justice of God to redress the injustices of this life, a desperate cry in the night of persecution and suffering. Death cannot have the last word!

It is in that perspective that the account of the resurrection of Lazarus (John 11:1–45) finds all its dogmatic force. The resurrection of Lazarus is a first entreaty addressed to God to manifest his power over death, but one must remember that the Resurrection of Christ is something else again. The latter is the passage to a new life, a life different from our mortal days. We are going to see that later on. For the moment, I would like to highlight just some aspects of this account which emphasise its place *before* the full light of Easter.

For here, faced with death, faced with Mary's pain, faced with the body which would already smell, Jesus was 'greatly disturbed in spirit, and deeply moved'. He wept (John 11:33–34). He who had just said with such sovereign certainty 'I am the resurrection and the life. Those who believe in me, even though they die, will live, and everyone who lives and believes in me will never die' (11:25). So why should he cry? He is the master of life, he is going to raise Lazarus from the dead. Why be disturbed in spirit, deeply moved, and weep?

The tears of a man are always disturbing. The tears of Jesus, a man of deep and delicate sensibility, open his heart to us. Does he sigh with anger in the face of 'these laments that are the expression of powerlessness and lack of hope in the face of death'? Verse 38 seems to authorise that interpretation, for it expresses the Jews' lack of faith and it is followed directly by the phrase, 'Jesus, again greatly disturbed'.

However, the Greek word used seems to mean in the context rather a sigh caused by a sort of invasion of sadness ('he is deeply moved'), which is exerted interiorly on the soul of Christ and which overcomes him entirely. Jesus' so human sensibility vibrates in harmony with the grief of Mary and Martha before the brutal fact of death. He shares their instinctive emotion, the repugnance of all flesh before its dissolution, for Christ is human. Like every man in the face of a death, he feels the icy touch of his own death. Even for him who believes that he is going to rise again, this passage remains formidable; it implies the destruction of the known, entrance into the unknown. One will find the same note in the fear that overwhelms Jesus in the Garden of Gethsemane. Do not believe that it was easy for him to accept death. Christ is not a bit like those insensitive heroes who face suffering cheerfully (sometimes through lack of imagination!). He bears within himself the ancient revolt, full of helplessness and grief, of innumerable generations of human-kind before the inescapable dissolution of their flesh. He experiences to the most intimate fibres of his being the burden of human death. There is a mystery here, as always when one would like to scrutinise the interior consciousness of Christ, a sort of coexistence of opposites. For Jesus brings in himself the victory over death, and he says it. 'I am the resurrection and the life' (11:25). I am the Resurrection because I am the Life. I do not possess the life – I *am* it. Neither I nor he who is identified with me by faith can be defeated by that negation of life which is death. Darkness cannot coexist with the light, or night in the presence of the sun.

And yet, he was weeping. Is it that the light was hidden from itself in some mysterious way, as when Christ feels abandoned by his Father, who nevertheless never leaves him alone? For Christ assumed the terrible truth of our death and our con-dition with its appearance of crushing finality.

The scene before the sepulchre of Lazarus is a sketch of the Paschal mystery: it is faith and life that triumph, Christ knowing that the Father always answers his prayer. Death is subject to his command: 'Lazarus, come out!' (11:43).

And Lazarus comes out. Here is one who returned from the mysterious land of the dead! What did you see, Lazarus? But he is silent, what is the use of speaking? Could we understand his words? Only silence can say something of what is on the other side.

The Saturday before we enter into the solemn contemplation of Passiontide, the Liturgy seeks to revive in us the thirst for God. We are poor, we have nothing – it doesn't matter! Our desire for the truth of life and death, that is our riches.

> Ho, everyone who thirsts,
>   come to the waters;
> and you that have no money,
>   come, buy and eat!

> (Isaiah 55:1 – Introt of Saturday)

And with what delicacy we are reminded that the whole gigantic drama at which we are going to assist, the life and death, of Jesus and of ourselves, are borne, enveloped, by the love of God. A love which Scripture can only express by evoking a hereafter of love full of tenderness, woven in the flesh of a mother for her child.

> Can a woman forget her nursing child,
>   or show no compassion on the child of her womb?
> Even these may forget,
>   yet I will not forget you.
> See, I have inscribed you on the palms of my hands . . .
>   (Isaiah 49:15–16a)

The Passion of Christ is the passion of Love.

PASSIONTIDE

16

A Mystery of Glory

**The standard of the King advances,
the mystery of the Cross shines out,
by which the Creator of all flesh
hangs in the flesh from the gibbet.**

It is a King who advances, a mystery of glory – 'beautiful, resplendent tree' – Christ the Saviour, although suspended from the tree, that the hymn of Passiontide presents to us. All our meditation on the Cross will be made in the light of Easter. We will not remain on the level of compassion for the sufferings of a man like us. We will embrace the mystery of Christ in all its dimensions, from the eternal Word of creation up to the final accomplishment of all things in God (1 Corinthians 15).

Instinctively, we sing this hymn more slowly, more solemnly. It makes us enter into the sanctuary of the mystery. The formulary of Sunday's Mass is more solemn, it expresses the prayer of the persecuted just man. The communion reminds us that the sufferings of Christ are 'for us', and invites us to enter into them through the memorial of the Eucharist. 'This is my body that is for you . . . This cup is the new covenant in my blood. Do this, as often as you drink it, in remembrance of me' (1 Corinthians 11:24–25).

In memory of Christ the Mass is always the memorial of the Passion, but it is so in a more poignant way during these days. During the last two weeks of Lent the Liturgy fixes our attention on Christ with an insistence more and more intent. So let us do likewise: 'Christ also suffered for you, leaving you an example, so that you should follow in his steps' (1 Peter 2:21).

Well, Lord, give me light, give me strength!

Therefore, since we are surrounded by so great a cloud of

witnesses, let us also lay aside every weight and the sin
that clings so closely, and let us run with perseverance the
race that is set before us, looking to Jesus the pioneer and
perfecter of our faith, who for the sake of the joy that was
set before him endured the cross, disregarding its shame,
and has taken his seat at the right hand of the throne of
God. (Hebrews 12:1–2)

The Liturgy does not offer us a didactic, logically ordered
treatise about Christ. It makes us enter into the living reality
of Easter by presenting us with the whole mystery of Christ,
successively evoked in his greatest prefigurations (Jeremiah, the
suffering Servant of Isaiah, etc.) and the interpretations of
the person and work of Christ (St John and the Synoptics, the
Letter to the Hebrews, St Paul). No picture fully grasps it, no
concept can express it, the Liturgy does not try to make the
synthesis. It places us before the reality of Christ; it permits us
to contemplate him, to unite ourselves to him by our love, to
be formed, in our heart, in his image. As I have already said,
let us not approach Christ as a subject to be analysed 'objectively', as a thing, or a dead man. Christ is alive, his mystery is
a current reality, and this reality is none other than our own
deepest reality. Only a heart that loves has the right to look
intimately at the countenance of another, for only love can see
the heart, that of Christ and ours. The face of Christ is the
face of Love, his mystery is totally a mystery of love. Christ is
a gift of love, a gift of the Father. Everything starts there.

In this is love, not that we loved God but that he loved us
and sent his Son to be the atoning sacrifice for our sins.
(1 John 4:10)

The texts of this time are so rich that I cannot quote or
comment on them all. I will just look briefly at some of the
great images of Christ, proposed by the Liturgy.

THE HIGH PRIEST

Christ, 'high priest of all the blessings which were to come' (Hebrews 9:11), puts a priestly seal on the whole of Passiontide.

At first glance, it is surprising that the letter to the Hebrews should present Christ as a priest. No other New Testament writing applies that title to him, and the Christ of the Gospels seems voluntarily to put himself in opposition to the Jewish priests as a class. The difficulty is only superficial, because it was precisely by going beyond and broadening the Jewish notion of priest that this title could have been applied to Christ, and that in terms, not of any religious activity, but in terms of his life, death and resurrection. The priestly consecration of Christ is his Passion and ascent into heaven.

The priest's role is to step across the distance between earthly humanity and the all-holy God, to establish a communion between them. Everyone is a sinner, and has a pardon to get and a purification to undergo. The Jewish priest, being himself a sinner, could not offer himself. He offered ritually pure victims in his stead. But 'it is impossible for the blood of bulls and goats to take away sins' (10:4). The liturgical action was only a sort of mime, powerless to transform interiorly or to grant access to communion with God.

That was clearly symbolised in the fact that the inner sanctuary of the Temple was closed to all except the High Priest, who entered into it once a year, furnished with sacrificial blood to make atonement for his sins and the sins of the people (9:7). The necessity to repeat this annual rite proved that it was ineffective.

The offering of Christ is quite different. It is not some object outside himself, it is the prayer that welled up out of his agony, it is his agony itself, assumed in obedience to the will of the Father and through love of us. It is not an external rite, it is the reality of his life and death. Christ offered himself, 'he entered once for all into the Holy Place, not with the blood of goats and calves, but with his own blood' (9:12).

He could offer himself and be accepted by God, because he was 'without blemish' (9:14). He embraced the human condition with all its distress: temptations, insults (11:26), suffering (5:8), death (2:9); he 'in every respect has been tested as we are, yet without sin' (4:15). 'Therefore he had to become like his brothers and sisters in every respect, so that he might be a merciful and faithful high priest in the service of God, to make a sacrifice of atonement for the sins of the people' (2:17). He was one of us, our brother; as a result of his solidarity with us, his sacrifice could save us (2:10–11).

The value of his sacrifice came from the fact that he was the Son and from the spontaneous gesture of his will, inspired by the Holy Spirit (9:14), by which he presented himself to accomplish with love the Father's will: 'In burnt-offerings and sin-offerings you have taken no pleasure. Then I said, "See God, I have come to do your will, O God" (in the scroll of the book it is written of me)' (10:6–7).

What was the Father's will? 'It was fitting that God . . . in bringing many children to glory, should make the pioneer of their salvation perfect through sufferings' (2:10).

Christ freely assumed our sufferings and human death, by a pure gesture of love for us and a perfect adherence to the love that comes from the Father, and by that fact, transformed them into sacrifices, into a passage to a new life, a life of communion with God. The humanity of Christ 'made perfect by his sufferings' (2:10; 5:9), entirely consecrated to God (John 17:9), passes to the world of the Resurrection. Resurrection is not to be understood as a simple, biological miracle, but as a spiritual transformation, which removes every obstacle to the divine life, which covers the distance between humankind and God. The risen body of Christ, 'the greater and perfect tent not made with hands, that is, not of this creation' (9:11), grants access to a true sanctuary in 'heaven itself' (9:24).

Our high priest really assumed our human condition to the end and he really sanctified it and raised it up to God, by his love and obedience. 'Jesus . . . [is] now crowned with glory and honour because of the suffering of death, so that by the grace of God he might taste death for everyone' (2:9).

His sacrifice is a sacrifice of covenant which lays the foundation for a communion of life between God and humankind.

On the one hand, an effective forgiveness of sins is now granted, since the blood of Christ purifies our consciences (9:14). On the other hand, the law of God does not remain outside us any longer: it is written on our hearts.

This is the covenant that I will make with them . . .
I will put my laws in their hearts,
    and I will write them on their minds.
(Hebrews 10:16 [Jeremiah 31:31–33])

By the grace of Christ, the desire to do what is pleasing to God and the power to accomplish it are implanted in us. Do we sufficiently remember this principle of life in us? We look for help outside ourselves, in medicine, psychology etc. We are in danger of clipping our wings and remaining at a human level, at the level of external rites. Only the divine power can lift us up as far as God, only the Spirit of Christ can form us in his image. And this power, this Spirit, are in our hearts. Let us enter deeply into our hearts by faith and prayer, let us be attentive to the voice of God in us and allow his Power to act.

The sacrifice of Christ is not a side issue of existence, but takes hold of his very existence, from his entrance into the world (10:5) up to his death on the Cross (2:14; 12:2). More exactly, it is that existence assumed in perfect adherence to the will of the Father (10:9), an adherence which at the time of the Passion is not realised without a dramatic entreaty (5:7–8). It was by a criminal's death, ritually 'impure', that Christ made the perfect offering which introduces human nature into God's intimate life. After that, we can see no part of human existence (except the act of doing evil), that has to be excluded from the relationship with God. All the separations and taboos fall. It is life that is the material of Christian sacrifice, all life without any kind of exclusion.

For this priesthood of life all Christians are constituted priests by the sacrament of Baptism, which incorporates them into Christ-priest. United to Christ, they have the power to make of their whole lives a sacrifice of praise to the glory of the Father. That is the fundamental Christian priesthood, it belongs to the realm of charity. The ministerial priesthood is at the service of that priesthood of life, because Christians need to renew their union with Christ and to immerse themselves in Christ's sacrifice made present through the ministry of priests. But what the Liturgy itself aims at is the transformation of the whole of life.

One can envisage the monastic life as the sustained effort to realise in truth this priesthood of life. That is why we say the following Scripture readings at Sext and None of the Sundays of Lent:

> I appeal to you therefore, brothers and sisters, by the mercies of God, to present your bodies as a living sacrifice, holy and acceptable to God, which is your spiritual worship. Do not be conformed to this world, but be transformed by the renewing of your minds, so that you may discern what is the will of God – what is good and acceptable and perfect. (Romans 12:1–2)

We will not envisage this offering of ourselves in terms of external sacrifices, but as the life of Christ in us, which wells up in our hearts, and puts our entire life in harmony with the will of the Father, and, by the Spirit of Love, informs every part of it.

> Therefore, my friends, since we have confidence to enter the sanctuary by the blood of Jesus, by the new and living way that he opened for us through the curtain (that is, through his flesh), and since we have a great priest over the house of God, let us approach with a true heart in full assurance of faith, with our hearts sprinkled clean from an evil conscience and our bodies washed with pure water [of baptism]. (Hebrews 10:19–22)

GRATUITOUS LOVE

Love does not want any other response but a response of love; so Christ wants in return for his love nothing else but ours. To put that love into deeds in the first place, like Martha, or above all exclusively, like the activists, would be to understand the revelation of love in a functional way, as a means to serve an end, for example, the salvation of humankind. That would be to fail to recognise that that love is that of a Person, and of an Absolute Person. God wants first of all our love for himself. Absolute Love should be loved and exercised by the lover; it demands an absolute response of pure adoration, pure thanksgiving which glorifies, and should inform our whole existence by giving it a meaning. It means giving unreserved priority to an attention, a receptivity without any other end but itself, apparently absurd from the earthly point of view, in the service of divine Love among all our occupations, however urgent and reasonable they may be (Luke 10:42). In that act of love and adoration which gives glory, we try to respond in a disinterested way to the love of God. It is only in the measure that this love exists and informs the Church's activity that that activity has a saving value for humankind.

So difficult to elucidate for the utilitarian mind, these truths are evident to the heart that loves. Love only wants love. In the Song of Solomon (the Song of Songs), the Bridgroom and the Bride have no children; they are totally for each other and they are enough for each other, and all fecundity is enclosed in the circle of that relationship.

> A garden locked is my sister, my bride,
> a garden locked, a fountain sealed.
>
> (Song of Solomon 4:12)

And nevertheless, the absolute response of love is filled with the conviction that that love from which all fecundity originates will be powerful enough to draw from the gratuitous gift every fruit pleasing to God in humanity and in the world. But that is God's business.

17

The Anointings of Jesus

Among the Gospels of the last two weeks of Lent, there are two accounts of an anointing of Jesus, once by 'a woman who was a sinner' (Luke 7:36–50), once by Mary of Bethany (John 12:1–2). The exegetes assure us that it is a question of two different people, and the meaning of each anointing is different. We are going to stop there, because these accounts wonderfully illustrate two aspects of our vocation.

The anointing by the woman of the town, told by Luke, is a scene of conversion and forgiveness. On the one hand there is the sinner who overcomes all thought of human respect to throw herself at the feet of Jesus, to kiss them, wash them with her tears, dry them with her hair and pour out perfume on them. The ardour of her repentant love shows the cold reserve of the Pharisees in its true light, and she deserves to hear these magnificent words:

> 'Therefore, I tell you, her sins, which were many, have been forgiven; hence she has shown great love. But the one to whom little is forgiven, loves little.' Then he said to her . . . 'Your faith has saved you; go in peace.' (Luke 7:47, 48a, 50)

To the sinner who is in each of us, this scene shows us the way to obtain forgiveness: the way of conversion, of compunction (the ancient monks would say), of tears for our sins, and above all, of love: to kiss the feet of Jesus will be to love Jesus himself and our brothers in him, for they are members of his body; to pour out perfume will be to sing our hymns of praise, to pray in the depths of our hearts, to sacrifice something precious and beautiful for love of Jesus.

It is not by chance that we read the account of the anointing by Mary of Bethany on the day following the first reading of the Passion (Palm Sunday). For here the spotlight is on the gratuitousness of a gift of great price – 'a pound of very costly ointment, pure nard' (John 12:3) – poured out in what seemed sheer waste on the feet of Jesus. The price of that perfume would have been better used by making gifts to the poor. But it is Christ himself who defends Mary's prodigality. 'Leave her alone!' He even says in another place that 'wherever this good news is proclaimed in the whole world, what she has done will be told in remembrance of her' (Matthew 26:13).

Whatever is done to the poor is done to Christ (Matthew 25:40); nevertheless, there is also a service of personal love to be rendered directly to Jesus himself; by consecration to the one thing necessary, the perfume of a pure heart, all the gifts and the grace of a precious life are thus withdrawn from the service of the members of Christ, in order to be poured out on the person of Jesus, in the gratuitousness of a direct love.

'The house was filled with the fragrance' (12:3). There is not in the Gospel an image as evocative of the effect caused by the hidden love which the contemplative life dedicates to Jesus as this image of a perfume that penetrates mysteriously and invisibly into every corner of that house which is the Church. We should not try to justify our vocation. That would already be a failure to recognise its true character. Beauty speaks for itself to him who has eyes to see. Love has no 'why'.

Jesus connects this action with his death: 'She bought it so that she might keep it for the day of my burial' (12:7). Honour is paid in anticipation to that body which is going to be nailed to the Cross. As if love, being unable to prevent that saving passage through death, at least surrounds it with its tender care and the marks of its honour. That is characteristic of the sensitivity of Jesus, who knew very well how to interpret the language of love's delicacy and to appreciate it.

The position of the reading of this Gospel after the reading of the Passion invites us, perhaps, to regard the renunciation of certain human purposes and satisfactions, implied in the act of pouring out the precious perfume of our life at the feet of Jesus, as a participation in the mystery of his Passion.

18

The Compassion of Mary

By the Cross her vigil keeping
Stands the Queen of sorrows weeping,
While her Son in torment hangs.

(Stabat Mater, trans. R. A. Knox)

Before contemplating the Passion of Christ, the Liturgy places us near the Cross in the company of the mother of Jesus, Mary Magdalene and St John. The heart of that mother, torn but renewing the 'fiat' of the perfect conformity of her faith to the will of God; the eyes of Mary fixed upon the reality of the crushed and bleeding body of the son of her flesh; the limpid and profound love of the Immaculate; the courage of that woman who followed her Lord up to the foot of the Cross, when nearly everyone was abandoning him – that is what we would need to have in order to contemplate the Passion of Christ.

'A sword will pierce your own soul too' (Luke 2:35). What a terrible hour for Mary, and what a test for her faith! For the Gospels do not authorise us to think that her situation was any different from that of the apostles before the light of the Resurrection dissipated the obscurity of their faith and allowed them to see the events from a completely different point of view. Suffice it to say that she suffered each of her Son's wounds as if in her own body and her own heart, that her faith held out, that she ratified the offering by Jesus of his life for us, thus 'in a wholly singular way, she co-operated . . . in the Saviour's work' and that thus 'she is a mother to us in the order of grace' (*Lumen Gentium* 61).

'Jesus . . . said to his mother, "Woman, here is your son." Then he said to the disciple, "Here is your mother" ' (John

19:26–27). Mary is our mother, for us who are the members of Christ. Let us put ourselves with her at the foot of the Cross, let us share in her compassion, to the extent of our love and faith and according to the depth of our 'fiat' to God's plan in Christ and in our life; we also will become 'co-operators with God' in the work of humankind's salvation. 'In my flesh I am completing what is lacking in Christ's afflictions for the sake of his body, that is, the church' (Colossians 1:24).

That verse has caused much ink to flow, and it is certainly not to be understood in the sense that the merits of the Crucified are not sufficient for the redemption of all people. The difficulty here is overcome by a more profound idea of the person of Christ who is not limited to the individual human nature which he assumed, but who also incorporates in his Person (though not hypostatically) all those who believe in him. We are 'in Christ', 'it is Christ who lives in us', St Paul will say; we are the vine shoots, Christ is the vine, St John will say. Incorporated into Christ, we enter into his Paschal mystery, our sufferings and our death sharing in the universal fruitfulness of his sufferings and death to the extent of our union with him. We lend him our liberty and our heart. Thus, according to the saying of Pascal, 'Jesus is in agony until the end of the world.'

All that was realised first of all in Mary, and with an intensity and to an extent never attained by any one else.

> Mother, fount whence love flows truest,
> Let me know the pain thou knewest,
> Let me weep as thou hast wept.
>
> Love divine within me burning,
> That diviner love returning,
> May thy Son this heart accept.

(Stabat Mater)

It is interesting that the first reading of the feast (Revelation 12:1–6a) puts before us the image of a great sign in the heavens, of 'a woman, clothed with the sun, with the moon under her feet, and on her head a crown of twelve stars' (12:1). It is she who was 'pregnant, and was crying out in birth pangs, in the agony of giving birth' (12:2), who after the ascension of Christ, 'escaped into the desert where God had made a place of safety ready, for her to be looked after' (12:6). Now, this woman refers first of all to the Church (see 12:17) and only secondarily to Mary as an exemplary member and mother of the humanity of Jesus. That is full of meaning, above all for us in whom the Church realises a physical presence in the desert. Like Mary, we give birth to Christ in our hearts and in the Church, to the extent that the Holy Spirit comes upon us, and that the power of the Most High covers us with its shadow (Luke 1:35). That shadow will be our compassion.

19

The Mystery of Suffering

The Servant of the Lord in Second Isaiah is the clearest prophetic description of Christ that the Word of God has recorded
in the Old Testament. The fact that the poems reveal to us
traits that are certainly personal, mixed with traits which seem
to indicate that it is Israel who is the Servant, or at least a
faithful remnant of Israel, does not surprise us. That antinomy,
unfathomable for the Old Testament, of the individual and the
group, has been resolved by the New Testament in the revelation of the total Christ, Head (Jesus) and Body (the Church)
and in all that which St Paul sums up by calling Christ a
second Adam (1 Corinthians 15:45). The Servant concerns us,
therefore; in one sense he is not only Christ, he is also us, in
Christ.

Above all, the realistic and vibrant language of the prophet
makes us face up to the suffering of Christ which our sins cost
him: it is for us that he suffered, his pain is the price of our
peace. It is the Christ of Grünewald, the crushed and tortured
body, that we are obliged to look at – and we do not like that.

At least, for my part, I don't like it. I find it hard to endure
the sight of another's suffering, above all that of someone I
love, like Christ. A feeling of indignation grows in me and even
sometimes a feeling of revolt against God, for it is God's justice
that demands that this man be thus tortured. With Job, I am
tempted to ask what our miserable sins, our tiny weaknesses
and failings can do to God who is so great, so transcendent, so
immutable, and beyond the reach of all suffering. And if there
is offence, wouldn't it be more magnanimous, more noble, to
forgive without demanding anything? He is Love, is he not?
Why take his revenge on humankind, above all on this man,
who, himself, was innocent? Why even take revenge at all?

Christ on the Cross forgave his torturers, he commanded us to forgive those who have offended us, saying that *that* is what it means to be perfect like our Father in heaven. Christ preached and gave the example of love, not of a strict justice. The demanding attitude of God towards humankind which obliges him 'not to spare his own Son' – how can one see in that the supreme testimony of the Father's love? So are those people right who offer themselves as victims to the divine Justice, to draw upon themselves, like lightning-conductors, the wrath of God which rages against sinners, who inflict all sorts of sufferings on themselves to please God, to appease him? Wouldn't that be quite a sadistic God? How could one love him? Was Ivan Karamazov (a character through whom Dostoyevsky expressed the atheistic rejection of God) right in refusing to have anything to do with that God, even if his personal eternal happiness is guaranteed him, if that implies the acceptance of a universal harmony which demands the suffering of one innocent child, of one single innocent child? And the suffering of Christ? Isn't that revolt more worthy of a human being, more 'just' than the justice of God? So, let him crush us, he is the stronger, but we will not say amen to his thirst for human suffering!

You will forgive me, you who are wiser than I, but it is good sometimes to express the rebellious thoughts that can coexist with more appropriate convictions. Evidently, cold logic would have no difficulty in detaching the sentimental element in these reactions and leading us to more complete views. One appears to be pleading the case of Christ-man against God, which is ridiculous. However, let us not forget that the relationship between God and humankind is a mystery which human intelligence, even in the light of faith, does not succeed in understanding completely. The dialectic tension at certain times (for example in the garden of Gethsemane) between the human will of Christ and the divine will; the errors of an unhealthy exaltation of suffering as such, of a certain dolorism whose pathological roots the psychoanalyst has every opportunity to show; the incontestable fact of the massive rejection by modern people of a God whose deformed image has been received from a superficial Christianity – all that invites us to a purification of our faith. How can I 'adore' the Cross, the instrument of execution of Christ whom I love? If it was the Cross, quite real, bathed with scarlet blood, the seat of torture of a being of flesh loved by you more than all the world, could you celebrate it, embrace it, adore it?

In my cell as a solitary, there is only one single image, the Crucifix and a little card of the Holy Face in sorrow. These things are always interrogations for me; they disturb me, they scorn everything that is reasonable to my human way of looking at things, they make me constantly go beyond my sensitivity and immerse myself in a mystery – which is a mystery of love. I dearly wish to believe it, but I scarcely 'see' it. All the same, on the occasion of this Holy Week, let us try to see a little more clearly, and to assume more profoundly that 'Fiat' which is the kernel of our faith.

MYSTERY OF FREEDOM

One can look at the Cross from two different points of view: as an act of God, or as a human act. The initiative belongs to God. God created us in a gesture of pure generosity, to make us share in his eternal Happiness. Only, we must enter into it as free beings in the image of our Creator. God respects our freedom to the point of allowing us to refuse his grace in a proud act of self-affirmation as an absolute value, and so, of refusal to obey. That produces an inner discord in us, and the entrance of suffering and death into humanity.

For all that, the love of God does not give up. Rather he takes the opportunity of humankind's fault ('O felix culpa', the Roman liturgy sings) to give him a greater gift, the gift of his only Son, who assumes our humanity in its mortal condition; but this time, in him, humankind conforms perfectly to the will of God by an act of obedience and love which carries our wounded nature through the trial of death, freely assumed in satisfaction for our sins, up to the very life of God. Thus the image of God is restored in humankind, our race is received before God in its Head, who, in giving us his own Spirit, gives us the possibility of reaching the world of the Resurrection, the world of eternal life. The consequences of sin remain, that is to say, suffering and death – because humans are beings of history, spread out over time; their past is them, in part. But the meaning of suffering and death has changed: formerly a final consecration of the failure of life, they become the place of humankind's passage to the Father in an act of free obedience and love, in the image of that of Christ, and by the power of that act of Christ present in us by his Spirit.

If God had simply blotted out our sin, he would, at the same time, have effaced our freedom. The suffering of Christ and his death, our suffering and our death, are the ransom of our freedom and the measure of our greatness – a greatness that we bear a little 'in spite of ourselves' at times!

JUSTICE AND SIN

On God's side also, his justice demands it. Yes, I say it indeed, his justice. But that justice of God must be understood well and not conceived of in the image of our petty human justice which is retributive. The justice of God, in the Bible, is a complex notion, but most of the time it refers to the mercy and fidelity of God, who seeks to lead humankind back to a 'just' relationship with himself, that is to say, who tries to get humans to become his friends and that by a gratuitous, saving act.

Let us not forget that God is Love; his justice is an attribute of Love, it is the justice of Love. However, the Bible also speaks of God's anger, a notion which concurs a little with our idea of vindictive justice. That embarrasses us today, and we tend to look at it as an element of progressive revelation now overtaken by the full light of the Gospel. But it is nothing of the sort. The same note will be found in the New Testament also. There is no alternative but to maintain an undoubted intolerance on God's part towards sin, an energetic rejection of evil.

We have a tendency to water down the notion of sin and, at the same time, not to grasp the true demands of love. Certainly, one must rectify the notion of sin: not to consider human weakness, carnal passions which are good in themselves, external religious practices etc. as priority issues, but to see the malice of sin in the refusal of Love who offers himself to us, in the consequent lack of love towards others; in the pride of the one who wishes to be an absolute, who does not accept obedience to a will superior to his own, who wants to be God and so, logically, wants the death of God. For that person, encounter with God is no longer a benefit. 'It is a fearful thing to fall into the hands of the living God' (Hebrews 10:31). For the sinner, Love is 'a consuming fire' (Deuteronomy 4:24) – precisely as Love, just as the light of the sun blinds the eye that is too weak, precisely by virtue of its luminosity. God is not a Grandpapa, benign and a bit feeble-minded. He is an ardent lover who gives himself totally and demands the total gift. He is light and cannot coexist with darkness. The holiness of Love is its ardour, incompatible with the coldness of refusal and indifference.

> 'I know your works; you are neither cold nor hot. I wish that you were either cold or hot. So, because you are lukewarm, and neither cold nor hot, I am about to spit you out of my mouth.' (Revelation 3:15–16)

We would be tempted to use this text in an argument a fortiori: all the more reason why God rejects sin. But the 'a fortiori' of the inspired text goes rather in the opposite direction: all the more reason why God rejects, 'vomits', the lukewarm – it is better to be straightforwardly a sinner than to settle into the bourgeois security, without greatness, of those who do not 'sin', but who do not love either. That speaks volumes about the 'psychology' of Love, does it not?

20

The Love of God

The love of God should not be situated principally on the level of felt emotions. For many, God seems to be distant, he does not evoke any emotional resonance. They do not love God less, if they venerate him as God and do his will. It is significant that it is St John, the great doctor of Love, who insists the most on the commandments: 'The love of God is this, that we obey his commandments' (1 John 5:3). By becoming man, God gave us an object more accessible to our emotions. By loving Christ, and our neighbour in him, we love God with our heart of flesh. But we must love them as Christ loved us, with a love that is gift of self and sacrifice.

He who sees Christ, sees the Father. Christ giving himself up to death for love of us – that is what the Father is like. He gave up what was most dear to him, his Son, who is the 'reflection of God's glory and the exact imprint of God's very being' (Hebrews 1:3), whom he loved with a love that is his eternal substance. Could he love us with such great love and remain beyond reach, immutable, in an icy transcendence, before our refusals, our sufferings, our death, before the suffering of his Son on the Cross? For my part, with Origen and a growing number of Christian thinkers, I do not believe it, although I know that one must immediately balance the assertion of a suffering of love in God with the assertion which is apparently contradictory, of the absolute transcendence and freedom of God towards his creatures. God is God, he cannot be likened to a piece among others in the creatures' game. However, it is not unthinkable that he should freely choose, through love, to enter into that game in a very real way. He can only be vulnerable if he wishes it himself. Nothing could constrain him to be so. But is that not precisely what he did by becoming man, and is the Incarnation not the expression of a choice of love, free and eternal, in the heart of the Father? Perhaps the deepest mystery is not that God loves us, for he is Love, but that he wants our love – for he is God.

It is not through anger that the Father delivered up his Son for us, but through love. One can decipher the sign of Christ only if one perceives, in the human gift of love that he made of his life, the manifestation of the Father's love, absolute love. The blood-stained face of Christ is the face of Love. He is not this sign by being a superman, but by being 'gentle and humble in heart' (Matthew 11:29) 'poor in spirit' (Matthew 5:3), obedient to the Father's will in order to bear the sin of the world (John 1:29) up to the point of dying on the Cross. That is absolute love, the unthinkable expression of the wholly other God.

That love is pure gratuitousness, before any response on our part. 'Christ died for us while we were still sinners . . . enemies [of God]' (Romans 5:8, 10). My faith is to believe in the existence of this love, not in perfect, abstract love as the philosophers would like to imagine it, nor in a universal love for my fellow humans as such. It is in this scandalous, irrational, gratuitous, absolute love of God in Christ that I believe.

> The life I now live in the flesh I live by faith in the Son of God, who loved me and gave himself for me. (Galatians 2:20)

Try to measure the full implications of our faith: the mystery of Being revealed as absolute Love who abases himself so far as to wash the feet and even the souls of his creatures, and who assumes in himself all the infamy of sin, all the hate which is relentlessly set against God, all the contempt which nails his unthinkable descent definitively to the Cross, and all that in order to excuse his creature before himself, in order to beg, to make his love possible.

It is faith in that love which leads us into the Kingdom where we are free to love. The rays of love penetrate deeply into our heart and effect our transformation; a response of love is born in us, a response which is a participation in that of Christ and which tends towards the perfection of that perfect human response to the divine love which gives us entry into the intimate life of God.

If it is true that 'it is no longer I who live, but it is Christ who lives in me' (Galatians 2:20), if it is truly Christ who loves in me, there will be, somewhere in my life, an absolute, gratuitous, irrational, scandalous love. To the extent of that love I am a Christian, a member of Christ, and not otherwise. To that extent also I will be able to understand 'the love of Christ which surpasses knowledge' (Ephesians 3:19). For love eludes all conceptualisation, all comprehension from without. It is the deepest mystery of being and of life, the intimate secret of myself and God, it only makes itself known to those who love.

> [May he give you the] power through his Spirit . . . that Christ may dwell in your hearts through faith, as you are being rooted and grounded in love. I pray that you may have the power to comprehend . . . and to know the love of Christ. (Ephesians 3:17–19)

21

The Kenosis of Christ

The implications of the prophecy of the Servant receive their full development in the great hymn (a very ancient Christian hymn) that Paul quotes, retouching it, perhaps, in his letter to the Philippians (2:5–11). It is not a question here of doing an exhaustive exegesis of it, it is so rich. I will merely present it in its essential movement which sums up the whole mystery of Christ.

> Let the same mind be in you that was in Christ Jesus,
>> who, though he was in the form of God,
>>> did not regard equality with God
>>> as something to be exploited . . .

> (Philippians 2:6)

It is a question of the historical Christ, God and man, in the unity of his concrete personality which Paul never divides, although he distinguishes his different states of existence. In this verse, Christ is considered in his pre-existence. He was literally in 'the form of God', that is to say, the visible figure which manifests the deeper being – the divine being of Christ is presupposed here. That state of equality with God was not regarded by Christ as a 'prey', an object of great price to acquire or retain. It is not a question of the divine being, which is not directly in question, but of the divine condition, equality of treatment, of manifested and recognised dignity.

> but emptied himself,
>> taking the form of a slave,
>> being born in human likeness.

> (Philippians 2:7)

He annihilated himself: from the Greek verb meaning 'to

empty, to despoil oneself' came the term 'kenosis'. This despoilment consists first of all in the very fact of the Incarnation: to become limited and mortal, to place himself in a state of inferiority to the Father. That thought disconcerts us, it is so difficult for us to realise that the Incarnation, far from being a game or a play, was the mysterious reality of a God whose divinity cannot be lost, yet who became a man as real as us. Christ remained God, but the glory which the divinity earned him by right and which normally ought to have been reflected onto his humanity – the Transfiguration only manifested the normal state of things – he chose to deprive himself of in order to receive it from the Father only as the prize of his sacrifice (John 8:50).

> You know the generous act of our Lord Jesus Christ, that though he was rich, yet for your sakes he became poor, so that by his poverty you might become rich. (2 Corinthians 8:9)

Christ took not only the human condition, sharing in all the weaknesses of that condition, except for sin, but he took the condition of Servant (or slave). It is a question of the Servant of Isaiah 52:13—53:12 (see 53:12b). Christ-made-man adopted a way of humility and obedience to the will of his Father; his role as Saviour will be fulfilled by vicarious suffering.

> And being found in human form,
>   he humbled himself
>   and became obedient to the point of death –
>   even death on a cross.
>
> (Philippians 2:7b–8)

He pushes obedience as far as death, a death on a cross reserved for criminals. This is the extreme point of his abasement.

> Therefore God also highly exalted him
>   and gave him the name
>   that is above every name . . .
>
> (Philippians 2:9)

Because of his obedience, God 'highly exalted' him, by the Resurrection and the Ascension. The Name that he receives is the name of Lord (see 2:11), the name used as a replacement for the unpronounceable name of God himself. To confer a name is to attribute not only a title, but a real dignity (Ephesians 1:21; Hebrews 1:4); so it is a question of the communication to the humanity of Christ of that which the divine Person renounced for itself. At the end of his earthly journey, Christ recovers, and this time for his whole being, including his humanity, the fullness of glory; from Servant he becomes Lord, and that, not by the way of honours, but by the way of humiliation.

The term 'highly exalted' implies, perhaps, an increase in comparison with what the pre-existent Christ possessed before; that could be the cosmic Lordship.

> So that at the name of Jesus
> every knee should bend,
> in heaven and on earth and under the earth,
> and every tongue should confess
> that Jesus Christ is Lord,
> to the glory of God the Father.
>
> (Philippians 2:10–11)

The whole universe, every creature, glorifies the One who humbled himself, and it is in the Father who exalted Jesus that this glorification culminates. Thus comes to rest the grand movement which, emanating from the eternal life of God, revealed the divine Lordship in Jesus, not in the glitter of power, but in the extreme humiliation of the Servant; then soared above the whole universe to reclothe the humiliated One with divine glory.

Remember that Paul here is not indulging in dogmatic speculations. He is proposing to us an example of humility for our imitation, an example which goes right against the spirit of acquisition and egoism that always aims at inflating the ego and achieving outward success, which is that of the old man in each of us. Christ invites us to poverty of heart, to radical dispossession with regard to our 'rights', to gratuitous self-giving, to the humility of obedience to the will of the Father. But the magnificent picture that Paul presents us with has no need of my moralising considerations. Look at this Christ: your heart will speak to you. For it is the heart of God that is open to your gaze, and how mysterious it is, how great it is!

TRIDUUM SACRUM

22

The Heart of Christ

The Liturgy takes on such a density for the Triduum Sacrum that I hesitate to speak of it: silence and the prayer of love are the only things adequate, for one is before the open heart of Christ. We have done our best to prepare ourselves; well then, let us immerse ourselves in the mystery of the Passion of Our Lord with a great love.

The texts are so rich! You understand that the rapid review I am going to give of the liturgy of these three days has no relationship to the importance of this liturgy.

HOLY THURSDAY

For me, this day has a quite special character, a beauty and a warmth the exact like of which I find nowhere else. That emerges above all from the last discourse of Jesus which we read at the Mandatum and during Mass. That is like a symphony of wonderful harmony, light, intimate, simple and so profound. If the musician St John left the mark of his contemplative soul on the words he relates, above all on their external form, it is the most intimate heart of Jesus that is his lyre and on which he plays. This is Christ in his supreme moment.

The ceremony of the washing of the feet, in its simplicity, translates into actions the humility of the Servant of God who becomes our servant for the love of God. The Prior is never as much Christ for us as at that moment. It is, for him, the sacrament of his responsibility as shepherd.

The memorial Mass of the Last Supper, anniversary, we say, of the institution of the sacrament of the love of Christ, has a limpid truth on this day. That love of Christ is present under an almost tangible form. He calls us his friends, his love penetrates our hearts of stone and changes them into hearts of flesh. In the shadow of the Cross he gives us his joy. His joy, born of the suffering of love, is stronger than suffering and death.

> 'I have said these things to you so that my joy may be in you, and that your joy may be complete.
> 'This is my commandment, that you love one another as I have loved you. No one has greater love than this, to lay down one's life for one's friends.' (John 15:11–13)

Born of the love of Christ, the law of our being, our truth, is to love – like Jesus. One with Christ, we are united among ourselves. The bread of his body which we eat, changes us into him, and makes us one single body. With the wine of his blood we are penetrated by the Spirit of his love.

GOOD FRIDAY

Suffering, above all, suffering which has a strong element of physical pain, is a mystery of solitude, a country into which one penetrates all alone. The greatest suffering of those who love him who is suffering is their powerlessness to follow him entirely. They can suffer with him to the extent of their love and their sympathy and sensitivity, and that creates a strong bond of communion between them. But there always remains an ultimate place where no one can penetrate. That applies in the highest degree to Christ, for the degree of suffering is measured by the depth of the soul, its capacity to love and its sensitivity. So who can join Christ in his suffering?

It is highly appropriate for us to spend the most of this day in the solitude of our cells. Thus we share Christ's solitude. It is not necessary to make long meditations nor profound reflections. All one has to do is to remain in peace and interior silence at the foot of the Cross, with our heart's attention fixed on Christ. Protestations, even of love, seem out of place, his suffering is so great. Simply to be there, that is all.

The reading of the account of the Passion is the 'sacramental' reading above all others. It is now that Christ is despised, wounded, nailed to the Cross, that he is abandoned by the

Father, that he is thirsty, that he dies. We are there. On the side of his persecutors or on Mary's side? Alas! Do I really know?

The great intercessions pour out over the whole world the grace and pardon gained for us on the Cross; as the blood and water that flow from the open side of Christ purify and revitalise the whole earth, this, humankind's poor earth which has such a thirst for them.

The Adoration of the Cross, barefoot, while the singing of the responses (I would say of the Suffering Servant) resounds in the sanctuary: I kiss the nailed feet of my Saviour and my God. What folly on the part of love is the Cross!

The silent communion in the body sacrificed for us.

HOLY SATURDAY

A day of expectation. Christ is buried, the Church remains silent in order the better to nourish her hope and faith in meditation and prayer. It is good to spend this day again in solitude, to enter into the mystery of Christ's descent into hell, a mystery which prolongs the humiliation of the Cross by manifesting the realism of Christ's death, when his soul truly experienced separation from his body. It is from the bottom of the abyss that he re-ascends to life. This descent already inaugurates his victory, for Christ descended towards those who were waiting for him, to proclaim to them their imminent liberation.

These days spent in solitude seem to me to reveal to us the most profound meaning of our solitude as monks. For that solitude is in its essence a participation in the mystery of Christ, in his redemptive solitude and in his communion of love with the Father in the Holy Spirit.

THE EASTER VIGIL

Easter night is par excellence the holy night, 'the mother of all holy vigils' (St Augustine). It interests us especially because the night vigil dedicated to prayer is an important part of our observance. The Easter vigil reveals to us the meaning of all our vigils, for it is the night in which the Church awaits the return of the Lord. She watches in expectation of the Bridegroom (Matthew 25:13) and nourishes her faith and hope by listening to the Word of God and by singing.

The culminating point of the liturgical year, this night is situated at the heart of the mystery of salvation. It manifests the two faces, death and resurrection, of this unique mystery and makes the link between them as Passover.

But the Church does not just recall the Passover of Christ, she celebrates it sacramentally, she renders present its mysterious efficacy. In this way, the mystery of Easter becomes the mystery of the Church, as its life-giving power passes from the Head to the Body. That is done in an eminent way by the two great sacraments which the Church associates with this vigil: Baptism, by which the mystery of the death and Resurrection of Christ is realised in the one who believes (Romans 6:38), and the Eucharist, memorial of that death and resurrection and the place of encounter with the glorified Christ.

The service of light
Christ is the light of our existence. To him we go, and him we follow. This is what we signify when we gather around the New Fire and when we enter into the church following the Easter Candle. We were in the shadow of death; Christ is our way out and our light within.

The church is illuminated with the Easter Candle at the lectern and with our candles. All is in the light, all bathes in the joy of the Resurrection. *Exsultet!* Rejoice! The whole creation, visible and invisible, rejoices, the Church rejoices. We are so used to knowing the outcome of the lying of Christ in the tomb that we forget the newness of the event of the Resurrection. But this is the Good News. Let us put ourselves in the state of wonderment at God's work. And let us truly give thanks to the Father with the deacon singing the *Exsultet*.

The Liturgy of the Word

Already, with the *Exsultet*, we have some clues about the way the Scriptures have been understood by the Christian community in the light of the Risen Lord. Now we go to the texts themselves. We pass in review the essential events of the history of salvation, as one casts a fresh glance back over the important stages of his life and understands them in a new and deeper way. The Creation, the Exodus, and the Eschatological Promise – but everything seen in the light of Christ. To enter into these readings, we should forget our rational mind and let our intuition speak. Everything works by images and symbols, by typology. Let us not be afraid to leap over the centuries and to connect up with the symbols used during the Easter Liturgy: light, water, bread.

In a way the prayers which follow the readings can help us, since the way they are shaped means they are constantly giving the readings a Christian application.

1. Genesis 1:1—2:2: Easter is an absolute beginning, a new creation of which Christ is the first-born, the new Adam of whom one becomes a member by Baptism. Humankind made in the image of God is re-created in the truth of that image by conforming itself to Christ, the Image of the Father. .

2. Exodus 14:24–31; 15:1: In the ancient Passover, the Hebrew people were liberated from slavery by passing through the Red Sea. It is through the waters of Baptism that the new people of God is saved.

3. Isaiah 55:1–13: All you who thirst for God, come, here is the water of the Spirit! The Lord concludes with us an eternal covenant, the Word of God transforms the heart of the believer.

4. Ezekiel 36:16, 17a, 18–28: That pure water which God promised to pour out on his people, the new heart which he promised to give, are brought into being in Baptism for the people of the New Covenant.

Then, four more readings, great christological texts of the

New Testament, which develop the mystery of Christ in all its fullness. Let us endeavour to capture a little of the wonder-struck joy of those first Christians; to be a Christian, in the glorious Christ, is so great! The first reading gives the tone from the very first verse.

5. 1 Peter 1:3–11, 18–23: 'Blessed be God and Father of our Lord Jesus Christ! By his great mercy he has given us a new birth into a living hope through the resurrection of Jesus Christ from the dead' (1:3). The Christian community is rooted in faith and love, it exults for joy, even though it may be in the midst of the worst trials.

6. Colossians 1:12–22: The greatness of Christ, the image of the invisible God, extends from the first moment of creation up to the last moment of time; it embraces the whole universe, all being.

> In him all things in heaven and on earth were created . . .
> For in him all the fullness of God was pleased to dwell,
> and through him God was pleased to reconcile to himself
> all things, whether on earth or in heaven, by making peace
> through the blood of his cross. (Colossians 1:16a, 19–20)

7. Ephesians 1:15—2:10: May God give us the light to understand the riches of our inheritance in the risen Christ, whose body is the Church, 'the fullness of him who fills all in all' (1:23); it is by grace alone that that is given to us.

8. Revelation 5:6–14: All the choirs of heaven unite their voices with ours to acclaim the Lamb that was sacrificed.

> To the one seated on the throne and to the Lamb,
> be all blessing and honour and glory and might
> for ever and ever.

                                                        (5:13)

What an impression of dazzling light emerges from these readings! The final response expresses it perfectly:

> It is the God who said, 'Let light shine out of darkness',

who has shone in our hearts to give the light of the knowledge of the glory of God in the face of Jesus Christ. (2
Corinthians 4:6)

There is a further development within the Liturgy of the Word.
With the singing of the Gloria the Easter candle leaves the
lectern in the nave to be transferred into the sanctuary, near
the lectern for the Gospel. For clearly the high point of the
proclamation of the Word is the solemn announcement of
the fact of the Resurrection, in the Gospel. 'Christ is Risen!'
Christ has triumphed, Life has triumphed. The Father has put
his seal on the life and death of Jesus.

Meanwhile a reading (Colossians 3:1–4) teaches us that the
Resurrection is not only the personal triumph of Jesus, it is also
our victory; already, from now on 'you are raised with Christ'.
Nothing seems changed in us and around us; suffering remains,
death remains. And yet everything is changed, everything is
new. The germ of a new creation is implanted in us, a leaven
which is going to transform us into Christ up to the day in which
it will bear fruit in eternal life. The cosmos itself is changed, it
is penetrated by a new hope. It is only just (to us living in
the Northern Hemisphere) that nature which was thrown into
upheaval by Christ's death (Matthew 27:51) should awaken at
this time; that she clothes herself with the beauty of smiling
flowers and green foliage, that she sings for joy through the voice
of the birds, that she pours out her kindness in the caressing
warmth of the sun. Christ is risen! Everything has a meaning,
everything has a hope, the promise of life is true in what it says,
the eternal aspiration of love will not be frustrated. That is the
good news.

From all the evidence, our risen life should be different. But
what should we be doing? 'Seek the things that are above,
where Christ is, seated at the right hand of God. Set your
minds on things that are above, not on things that are on earth'
(Colossians 3:1–2).

'On high' and 'below': these are images. One could equally
say 'within' and 'without'. The meaning is that, immersed in
the new life of Christ, the world of earthly realities by itself is

no longer sufficient. We are made for something else, for a life of eternal love in Christ. That is our goal. All our efforts should be directed towards that goal. What else is monastic life but that?

We are marked, we have become different. 'For you have died, and your life is hidden with Christ in God.' Our true life is the life of the risen Christ which flows in our arteries as baptised people. And that life is hidden – in God, but hidden all the same. Only the eyes of faith can grasp it, and only in the dark.

What a strange life we share in! How profound the mystery of our Christian being is: 'We are God's children now; what we will be has not yet been revealed' (1 John 3:2a). Our being of grace is a reality of hope, a dynamic stretching out towards the realisation of what is already there in an inchoate, veiled manner. It is not a question of an organic development, as for a plant. The life in us is a life of love and knowledge, it is a personal life par excellence, for it is the participation in the life of him who is Life, Truth and Love. Our life has a name, it is Christ. It was born of an historical event, the death and Resurrection of Christ. It will reach its fullness in another historical event, the return of Christ in the last times.

> When Christ who is your life is revealed, then you also will be revealed with him in glory. (Colossians 3:4)

> We will be like him, for we will see him as he is. (1 John 3:2b)

Thus whispers the man of prayer. The obscurities of contemplation here below will one day be dissipated. Not only will we see Christ, but we will be transformed into him, that is to say, we will at last be ourselves. 'Come, Lord Jesus!'

After this reading, we recall, the Liturgy intones the first Alleluia of Easter, the Christian's shout of triumph:

> O give thanks to the Lord, for he is good;
>   his steadfast love endures for ever!

> (Psalm 118:1)

In the joy of Easter, with a true instinct, it is the love of the Lord, not his power, nor his justice, that the Church celebrates. For the Resurrection is the power of eternal life, of love. On this holy night the Resurrection seems to me joy, peace, hope; light that rises up out of the darkness of the night; a totally new faith, wonder-struck and timid, but nevertheless stronger than death. That beauty to which I thrilled, that tangible yet elusive love, those inexpressible things that I have guessed at and that have touched me lightly in passing, all that, one day, will rise up out of the dust of my flesh to be eternally, and that will be Christ. It is madness, but I believe in it, my God! And even if I am wrong, I am right nevertheless. Without this infinite horizon, I would no longer be a man. If love does not have the last word, if it is not eternal, nothing has meaning.

The Baptismal Liturgy
With the Service of Light, this is another rite that finds its full meaning on this night. It is highly significant that the Liturgy places here the renewal of the baptismal profession of faith. When there is Baptism of adults, it is celebrated here. This fits in also with our religious profession, which is nothing other than a way to live our Baptism fully. So we renew at this point our adherence to Christ and our renunciation of everything that is opposed to that. The preceding readings stated very precisely the object of our faith. Therefore, may our act of faith be profound and truly commit us.

The water is blessed and sprinkled on each of us 'in remembrance of our Baptism: that God may keep us faithful to the Spirit we have received'; that we may be protected from the attacks of Satan; that our heart may be purified and the source of grace in us revived.

The Eucharistic Liturgy
It was in the breaking of the bread that the disciples recognised the risen Christ (Luke 24:35). On the road he remained unknown. In the thanksgiving and sharing, he made himself known.

We have seen that the apostolic Church did not separate

Baptism and the Eucharist. Re-immersed in Christ and in the community of the Church by the renewal of Baptism, we realise our union with Christ and with our brothers in the most intimate manner in the celebration of the memorial of Christ dead and risen. The risen Christ is present among us, we receive him into our bodies and into our hearts; in him and through him we are intimately united to our brothers, in his love, and in the one life in which we are immersed.

Is it on this night that he is going to return in triumph? For the first Christians it was a moment of intense expectancy. But perhaps he has come and and we have not recognised him – in our brothers, in our faith and hope? His triumph is perhaps the humble charity realised in the communion and the concelebration of the Mass, which brings out so well the union of priests and faithful in the one priesthood and the one sacrifice of Christ. Basically, what is the Parousia? What is time?

Lauds

The lyrical praise of Lauds expresses our genuine need in our joy – we need to adore! We need to sing! Alleluia! The Scripture reading sums up the whole mystery.

> . . . just as Christ was raised from the dead by the glory of the Father, so we too might walk in newness of life.
> For if we have been united with him in a death like his, we will certainly be united with him in a resurrection like his. (Romans 6:4b–5)

Back in cell

We leave the church to go back to our cells carrying our lighted candles. With Christ in us, 'the hope of glory' (Colossians 1:27), we are transformed, unified, become like him, that is, men of 'the eighth day', of the New Creation, risen. As such we are not separated from all and confined within the four walls of our cells, but on the contrary our hearts expand into infinity. Let us be sure that we can already be granted what Evagrius Ponticus said of the man of 'the eighth day':

Separated from all, he is united to all;
Impassible, yet of supreme sensitivity;
Deified, he counts himself as the world's refuse.
Above all he is happy,
Divinely happy . . .

EASTER

23

Alleluia!

Alleluia! Praise the Lord. The Lord has done great things for us. I would like to make some very simple remarks about the Resurrection. This is at the centre of our faith: without resurrection, our faith is vain. If we have believed for this life only, we are the most wretched of men. But what is the Resurrection for me?

The Resurrection is repose after the painful tension of the Passion, it is the stone rolled away from the tomb, it is the joyful cry of Mary Magdalene, it is the other side of death, become luminous. It is the certainty that life is already triumphant and that it will triumph in the end: the fundamental force that sustains the world and history is love, and love is stronger than death. It is only in the light of the Resurrection that I understand what life is.

In the Resurrection of Jesus, God manifests the power of love, a power that cannot be limited even by suffering, failure or death. The Father of Jesus is the God of the living; by our faith in Jesus we are children of God, and consequently living beings. What we are already will be manifested later, when the sentence of our life here below will be completed by the verb of death in order for the phrase to signify, paradoxically, life.

He whom God loves, God has made one with him, and he will make him eternal with him. He will not leave his friend in the darkness of death. And he has manifested in Jesus, in his death and Resurrection, the extent to which he loves us. The risen Jesus is the first-fruits of love; we will follow him, for through faith his Spirit dwells in us, that Spirit who by his divine power has raised him from the dead.

In that sense I am, we are, already risen; a seed of indestructible life is sown in our hearts, a love stronger than death is given to us, here and now. Already, this love is doing the work of love in us; it gives us the desire and radical possibility of loving, and assures us that every work of love is eternal. Nothing will be lost, neither the smallest smile, nor the most insignificant gift, nor the effort most deeply inscribed in space and time. The flower of one day exhales an eternal perfume before God.

It is Jesus in the totality of his humanity who is raised up by God, not only his soul, the spiritual dimension of his being, but his body also, the dimension of his being that is incarnate in matter. It will be like that for us also. How, I do not know. In what state precisely, I do not know. It matters little. If the resurrection opens, not onto a prolongation of this mortal life, but onto a new, different life, it will have to be a mystery for me. It is a question of the work of the mercy of God par excellence; we are related to God himself, because the life of the resurrection makes us participate in the divine life itself. There, everything is transfigured by that dazzling power of life and love which is God, and consequently, to our mortal eyes, everything is mysterious – and nevertheless so close at times, behind the diaphanous curtain. It is not on my understanding that I can rely, but only on God himself alone.

I place my life, my desire, my hope, and the life, desire and hope of all my brothers, of all creation, in the hands of Love, and my eyes fixed on the paradox of the all-powerful Crucified One enable the depths of my heart to rest in an unshakeable confidence and optimism.

Nothing is absurd, nothing is without reason. Everything is governed by a vast intelligence. Even the misuse of our liberty is redeemed and becomes the opportunity for a greater good. We do not even have to fear our own sin, provided there is repentance. The heart of God is deeper still, his love is gratuitous, his gift of himself without condition. Nothing can separate us from the love of God in Jesus Christ.

We can look death in the eye. The Lord has assumed and subjugated death. He who is the Beginning and the End made an eternal beginning out of a temporal end. We can confront the sufferings of this life, our own and that of others, without despairing. In the Father's Kingdom every tear will be wiped away, every thorn will be revealed clothed with a rose. There at last, justice will reign, the humble will be exalted, the pure of heart will see God. Happy the poor, that kingdom is theirs.

And we are all poor people. Little by little we become aware of that: poverty and solitude are our lot. We are always alone in the face of death and suffering – alone except for the Father, our Father, who sees in secret with a loving gaze. What is there to do, before the terrible greyness of the human heart – our own heart, that of others? In the face of its pettiness, its egoism and its futility, what is there to do? Believe in Christ, hope against all hope, love as much as one can, allow the power of the Spirit to act in us, trust in God, trust in the faith of our brothers, begin again untiringly every day, seek with Easter eyes, cultivate with all our care the seeds of light and love that cross our lives and those of our brothers, have the courage of a joy that no one can take away, the serenity of a peace born on the Cross, the humility to receive everything, gratuitously, without any merit.

The Father assumed all, suffered all in his Son. The Spirit can transform all into life by his love; nothing escapes him. In the Risen Christ the sun is already risen, and we are the sons of that light. This is the Lamb that was sacrificed, who sits at the right hand of the Most High. May our morning joy be an echo of the Father's joy. May no reflection on our unworthiness put a stop to its impetus. This is not important. Our adoration raises our eyes towards the Lord who is Love, who alone is.

Let us break together the bread of our sinful humanity, so that Jesus may be able to walk with us towards the Father's inn. May our fraternal solitude sustain each other in mutual forgiveness and a single hope, while we walk, humbly and joyfully, towards the love which summons us from within towards the Father.

And may our thanksgiving, assumed in the Thanksgiving, the Eucharist of Christ, be constant and strong. Alleluia! Praise the Lord, for he has done great things for us. Eternal is his love and eternal the gift of his love in the risen Christ.

Alleluia!

24

An Easter Reflection

He is there, the Lord, beside us, the same and yet different. He takes part in our usual activities, he watches the fishing, he eats with us around the fire, he walks with us along the road, he explains the Scriptures to us, he shares our bread. But he has changed, and at first we do not recognise him. Then, a familiar gesture, a word, and we recognise him, it is he! Rupture and continuity with Jesus of Nazareth. He bears the marks of the nails in his hands, but he is Lord and God; to him all power in heaven and on earth is given.

We hesitate, we hang on to the familiar contours of the sadness that followed the ruination of our hopes. It is painful, but it is within our reach, 'we are well-versed in it'. Our egoism knows how to draw nourishment even from suffering, and our fear uses it as an excuse in order to withdraw into a bitter solitude, crowned by the vainglory of the 'martyr'. Can we give ourselves up to this joy that disorientates us, makes us enter into such an intense light? He who hoped, who wanted to love, who for a moment looked towards a happiness that was too high – that man is dead. Why disturb him with your light that is too pure, your life that is too strong, your love that is too demanding? If we agree to believe – again! – to what suffering, to what disappointment are we opening the door? We will be changed, everything will have to be begun again, we will be obliged to open our heart, to throw ourselves into a life of love, and suffering lies in wait on the road. Surely it is only our thwarted desire that wants to make us see Christ alive. It cannot be true. It is too beautiful! Or is it too hard for our selfishness, for our fear?

Nothing is conclusive. An apodictic proof of the Resurrection cannot be given. No one saw Christ rise from the dead. The apparitions could be illusory. The empty tomb does not prove much. One believes in the Resurrection or one does not believe in it. (Of course, our faith is reasonable: it is supported by good reasons, but these reasons do not constrain, as for example in the case of a mathematical reasoning.) Let us not believe too easily! A dead Christ leaves the world to us – a world that does not amount to much, but is within our reach. A living Christ, present – that changes everything. One no longer knows where the limits of the universe are. It opens onto an abyss from all sides. We are no longer sufficient to ourselves. We are obliged to walk in the obscurity of faith. We are marked, each and every one of us, by the Cross. Love lies in wait for us. We are too big.

THE LORD SPEAKS

'Peace be with you.' You still do not understand? Death, darkness, suffering, egoism, your limitations, your weakness, your sin – all that is defeated, once for all. I did not just return to the life I had before my death. I have passed into the Kingdom of the Father, into the true life, which is eternal and indestructible, a life of love and communion, of light and praise, which is quite different from the life of your world, although it does respond to the secret desire of beginners for that life. I have entered into the glory of the Father, that glory which I possessed from all eternity as Word, and which, by my death, reflects now onto my humanity, so that I, the man Jesus, with the Father, from the fullness of our love, I am the source of the divine Spirit which I send upon you and on all people. ' "I am the Alpha and the Omega", says the Lord God, who is and who was and who is to come, the Almighty' (Revelation 1:8).

Do not be afraid! It is not a high ideal or a lofty moral standard that I put before you and that you know yourself to be quite incapable of realising. I am not lecturing you. I know you too well. Agreed, you are a sinner, you are worthless, you don't know how to love or do great deeds. But don't you understand? That has no importance. I love you exactly as you are. I have taken your weaknesses upon myself, I shared them, all except your sin. Let us not speak about it any further. All that is defeated, finished. 'But, Lord . . .' Be quiet and listen a moment, will you? How slow you are to understand! You are going to say that nothing in you seems changed. But, yes, everything is changed, at a deeper level than that where you usually look. Yes, you are going to pass through suffering and death, but that will now be, precisely, a passage to that true life of which I was speaking just now. Your weaknesses remain, so that my power in you may appear as coming from me and your pride may not appropriate it. The effort, the risk, the responsibility of your freedom remain, so that you may be a man, that you may come to me of your own accord. I want you to have a share in my entire mystery, not only in my glory, but in my laboriously lived love and in my death. In that way, life will pass through you to your brothers. Your powerlessness to love truly with all your heart, that will also remain, but only to the extent that you must learn to climb the road of love, as a human being, a creature who makes himself, little by little, and above all, to the extent that you still have not learned not to count on your own strength to love, so that you let me love in you.

For that is the ultimate answer to all your doubts. What I bring you is the gift of my risen life, my light which sees the Father face to face, my love which is the love of the Father in me and my love in the Father; a love which is the bond of communion in the Trinity of God, and between you and all your brothers in my body, the Church. You have only to open up by faith so that the divine power of this light-life-love may unfold freely in you. It is not measured by your weakness but by my power. It is by contact with my glorified humanity that this life is given to you. The Spirit wells up from my human heart (John 7:39). And in and through my glorified body, it is everything human, with its particular nature and finiteness, that enters into Life – not a smile will be lost; it is the human in the precise contours of its ephemeral reality that enters into eternity, that will live for ever. Not only the human but everything created: that beauty of a day is eternal. All the poets glimpsed that, for that matter. Do not shut me up within the limits of a body like yours in its present condition. My glorified body is enlarged to the dimensions of the whole universe; my glorified life is its secret sap, and my Spirit its transforming heat.

Everything is going towards the goal, the Parousia, when everything will enter into my glory and God will be all in all. Let yourself be carried, tiny piece of pusillanimous poverty. Give me your empty space to pour into it the vitality of my love and my joy. Believe in joy – it is possible, even for you. Believe in love. Believe in life, in true life. Believe in me, because I love you. Be my joy in the heart of the Church. (That is a definition of Carthusian life which is as good as any other, it seems to me.)

The meaning of life, the meaning of time, is to strain towards that final victory, not to realise it fully in your life. For you also must follow the humble way of the Servant. You will walk in the obscurity of faith along a hidden way. Your glory – my glory in you – you possess in hope. You will be a man of desire, a pilgrim borne along by the joy of the homeland that he feels in his heart. A poor man, rich in love, in my love for you. I give you my poverty: be my love. Love! That is the substance of eternal life. It is already present because I am present, to the extent of your faith and your love.

Come, Lord Jesus!

25

The Faith of Mary Magdalene and Thomas

'My Lord and my God!'

(John 20:28)

'Blessed are those who have not seen and yet have come to believe.'

(John 20:29)

In order to illustrate the nature of our relationship with the Risen Christ, St John, in the twentieth chapter of his Gospel which describes the post-Easter apparitions, makes two figures stand out: Mary Magdalene in the first part (20:1–18, read on the Thursday within the Octave of Easter) and Thomas in the second part (20:19–29). These two sections are put together in a similar manner.

Mary, at the start, weeps at the sight of the empty tomb; Thomas doubts the reality of the risen Christ. Mary makes her confession of faith when the Lord reveals himself to her, just like Thomas when the Lord appears to him. In both sections the fact of physically touching the Lord is brought out, with a note of very human sensibility. Moreover, her faith wins for Mary Magdalene the mission of announcing the Resurrection to the disciples, while Thomas's confession precedes the faith of those who have not seen.

Finally, throughout the whole chapter it is a question of passing from the physical experience to spiritual faith: the beloved disciple believes on seeing the cloth and the linen wrappings (20:8), Mary when the familiar voice of the Master pronounces her name (20:16), the disciples when they contemplate the hands and side of the Lord (20:20), Thomas when he is allowed to see Christ's hands and put his hand into his side (20:27). Thomas's faith precedes the faith of all the believers in the future (20:29) whose faith will rest not on vision, but on the testimony of those who have seen.

> What was from the beginning, what we have heard, what we have seen with our eyes, what we have looked at and touched with our hands, concerning the word of life . . . we declare to you what we have seen and heard so that you also may have fellowship with us; and truly our fellowship is with the Father and with his Son Jesus Christ. (1 John 1:1, 3)

The faith of the Church is applied to the glorified but real humanity of Jesus. That is not an abstraction, a gnosis, but a reality, a concrete history. However, the act of faith goes further than the physical reality put before our sensory eyes; it reaches the divinity of Christ through his glorified body. 'My Lord and my God!' The sensory presence of Christ can be replaced by the sole testimony of those who have seen him, the act of faith retains all its power to reach God. It can even be purer. 'Blessed are those who have not seen and yet have come to believe.'

After the period of the apparitions, there is the time of faith that does not see, that is deprived of the sensible presence of the Lord. It is our time. St Peter does not see that as a misfortune – far from it:

> In this you rejoice, even if now for a little while you have had to suffer various trials, so that the genuineness of your faith . . . may be found to result in praise and glory and honour when Jesus Christ is revealed. Although you have not seen him, you love him; and even though you do not see him now, you believe in him, and rejoice with an indescribable and glorious joy, for you are receiving the outcome of your faith, the salvation of your souls. (1 Peter 1:6, 7b–9)

Faith should know how to hold firm in trial, should know how to prefer what is invisible, what is only possessed in hope, to what directly strikes our sensibility. 'Now faith is the assur-

ance of things hoped for, the conviction of things not seen'
affirms the letter to the Hebrews (11:1). And Paul continues:
'For in hope we were saved. Now hope that is seen is not
hope. For who hopes for what is seen? But if we hope for what
we do not see, we wait for it with patience' (Romans 8:24–25).

In the spiritual life, there is often at the beginning a time of
sensible presence on the part of Christ who allows the soul to
see something of his glory and to taste his joy. The reality of
our union with Jesus is nearly palpable and sweeps everything
along. Sacrifice is done cheerfully, prayer is full of light and
delights, love for one's brothers happens without effort, the
action of the Spirit is felt as an active force.

All that is necessary. We are so poor that at the beginning
we can really love only what brings us some comfort. To turn
us away from the visible objects that we love so much, our
sensibility must be attracted by an enjoyment within its reach,
an enjoyment it can feel. But that entails imperfections: one is
in danger of loving God for his gifts and not for himself. One
is in danger of thinking that the knowledge afforded by that
grace, the lights, the relish, the sweetness, even the vision (!),
give us God as he is – when in reality there is no proportion
between these effects in our sensibility and God himself. Then,
the soul seeing itself satisfied – and at times abandoning itself
greedily to its enjoyment – is in danger of becoming conceited,
believing itself to be different from others, although in a very
subtle way (one can even take pride in one's great humility!).
Finally, one's sensibility is so linked to the instinctive, natural
life, that the action of grace through it involves a certain mixture
of ambiguous elements.

In short, after a time, the grace whose effects can be felt,
even if authentically given by God, can become a screen and
bar the way which ascends towards him. If that is true of
the physical presence of Christ's humanity with regard to the
Apostles, how much more is it true of the graces that affect our
feelings?

MARY MAGDALENE

You recall that Jesus formerly praised the gesture of the woman who was a sinner (it is likely that Luke identifies her with Mary Magdalene), who threw herself at his feet and covered them with kisses (Luke 7:36–50). But after the Resurrection, when Mary Magdalene, recognising the Master, took hold of Jesus' feet, putting the impetuosity of her love into that gesture, the Lord pushes her away: 'Do not hold on to me, because I have not yet ascended to the Father' (John 20:17).

Christ has not yet ascended for Mary Magdalene. Her love leans too much on Christ's humanity; it relies too much on the senses, it is still too limited. However, an essential change has occurred and Jesus no longer allows the contacts of the past. Between the two gestures of Mary Magdalene, the Passion and Resurrection have occurred. At first, Mary Magdalene had not understood the meaning of the Resurrection. Having discovered the tomb open, she ran to tell Peter and John. They came, they saw the empty tomb, the linen wrappings in place. John, at least, believed. But as for Mary Magdalene, she remained outside. She was weeping. She only saw the absence of Christ's body. 'They have taken away my Lord, and I do not know where they have laid him' (20:13). Christ himself has to call her by her name, 'Mary!', in that tone that reveals the One she loves, for her eyes to be opened: 'Rabbouni!' One notices that the Resurrection has not at all blurred the inimitable and individual character of the Lord's relationship with his friends. It is indeed Jesus.

However, the intimacy and familiarity of love are no longer realised in the same way nor at the same level. Mary will no longer be able to kiss Jesus' feet – she must hold Christ with the grasp of faith which alone is capable of embracing the Lord of glory in all his greatness, within a union more intimate and close than when she touched him with her hands.

Instead of touching him from outside, by the gift of faith and the Spirit that Christ sends, she becomes *one* spirit with him, *his* love enters into her, *his* life animates her, she becomes one with him to the point of sharing his very being. And at the heart of this union with Christ, Mary Magdalene is united to her brothers, to everyone, in an internal love, in the Spirit who touches and transforms her being. Her love espouses the dimensions of the Spirit and transcends the limitations of sensible contact; having become the love of Christ in her, it increases until it envelops all people without the limitations of time and space; she touches them, loves them, there where the Risen Christ touches and loves them, in the depths of their heart.

So, like Mary Magdalene, all those who love Christ with her must agree to this deprivation and this deepening of their manner of loving. Maybe that will not happen in one day, nor without trouble and suffering, but it will happen to the extent that Christ, the mystery of Christ's love, lives in them.

THOMAS

The transcending of the sensed presence that happens in Mary Magdalene in the purification of her love, along a feminine register, happens in Thomas in the purification of his faith, along a masculine register.

It is indeed in the style of St John to concentrate the doubts and hesitations of the disciples before the fact of the Resurrection into a single character. Thomas's personality is well characterised already in the Gospel. He is a quite difficult character, our Thomas, a man who is very cut and dried, independent, who judges things in his own way and does not enter easily into the mind of another: 'Lord, we do not know where you are going. How can we know the way?' he asks, with a touch of impatience, during Jesus' farewell discourse (John 14:5). No mysteries, say things clearly, for goodness sake! Besides, he is basically generous and loyal in his own 'realistic' way. When Lazarus' death is made known, it is he who cries: 'Let us also go, that we may die with him' (John 11:16). So much the worse for us, but we will follow the Master to the end!

Thomas was absent at the time of Jesus' first apparition on Easter day, and to refuse to believe the testimony of his brothers is quite in accordance with his temperament. 'Unless I see the mark of the nails in his hands, and put my finger in the mark of the nails and my hand in his side, I will not believe' (John 20:25). He will only trust the evidence of his own senses. He is an individualist, quite mistrustful and sceptical by nature. Let all the others believe – that is their business. He is not influenced by the opinion of the masses. As for him, he wants to verify, by seeing and touching, that Jesus is really risen.

Eight days later, Jesus offers him that possibility. 'Put your finger here and see my hands. Reach out your hand and put it in my side', and he adds, 'Do not doubt but believe' (20:27). Bowled over, 'Thomas answered him: "My Lord and my God!"' (20:28). Typically, he who has resisted faith the longest, once won over, in a single burst goes further than all the others. Up to then, no one in St John's Gospel had yet given that title to Christ. In a spontaneous way, Thomas expresses in it his total belief in the divinity of Christ.

Jesus does not praise Thomas. His hesitation, his 'materialism', if you like, his act of faith, had a providential value of testimony for all the sceptics of all ages, but he is not, for all that, proposed as a model to be followed. 'Do not doubt but believe.' Thomas should have done without his demands for tangible evidence. 'Blessed are those who have not seen and yet have come to believe' (20:29). Beatitude is promised to all believers who have not been eye-witnesses to the facts reported, to all the future Christians who will compensate by the ardour of their faith for what they lack of Christ's visible presence.

Become a man of faith

But there is something of Thomas in each one of us. The act of faith is not made once for all. We are obliged to renew it each day, in every choice, in every decision. And we often demand proofs from Christ. We want to see, to ascertain his presence, his providence, his love. To walk in pure faith is difficult for us, always difficult. And nevertheless, that is the true desert, the rest is only a framework.

The monk's life is essentially a life of faith, or it is nothing. The monk is a man of faith or he is a fool. The whole spiritual edifice is based on faith, faith that is the first gift of God's love. We have to learn little by little to see everything, to evaluate everything with the eyes of faith. We must know how to transcend the myopia of our senses and our human intelligence to penetrate into the deeper reality of creation, of events, ultimately of the intimate life of God. We must know how to renounce sensible happiness in favour of that fullness of life and joy that faith reaches.

Our union with God is not measured by its sensible resonance in us – that can be non-existent at times – but by the depth of our faith and our spiritual love. The quality of our prayer is not measured by the enjoyment at the level of the senses or by the special lights it gives us, but again by our faith and spiritual love. A prayer all reduced to essentials, a presence to God in a calm, simple, imageless, spiritual act of faith, and in an act of love that is a peaceful and total abandonment of the heart to the will of God and a desire to love him in everything and above everything and to do his will in everything, in spite of a more or less total absence of felt satisfaction – that prayer can be more true than a prayer full of emotional fervour. Not that our sensibility has not its place in our relationship with God. Our heart is a heart of flesh, and it is normal that it should vibrate 'fleshly' to the love of God. We need the impetus of our passions in order to love God and our neighbour. Only, our sensibility needs to be purified, perhaps even 'lost' for a time, to allow us access to a purer love and faith which is more spiritual, beyond the reach of the fluctuations of our sensibility, based on more stable and deeper foundations. Afterwards, if God wishes it, we will recover the riches of a sensibility that will be the faithful lyre of a spiritual love and faith. As Abraham recovered Isaac.

But we will know how to distinguish the essential from the accidental: we will know how to build our spiritual life on faith. In prayer, we will know that it is useless to weary ourselves in artificially arousing our emotions, and to believe that we are abandoned by God if we feel nothing towards him. We will put ourselves before him in an act of pure faith and simple love. That is the essential.

The solitary above all should get used to living in the peace of a rather bare and spiritual faith. He should seek that, as he instinctively seeks the pure, fresh air of the mountain, the profound silence of the desert. And he will be surprised to discover that that purity enables one to find God in his elusive presence. That solitude, at times painfully felt, is a deeper, more precious communion: the serene gaze of a heart to whom it suffices to be love. That silence is a lighter, more beautiful song than any other.

26

Bodily Exercises

This evening, instead of talking about the Resurrection, we are going to try, as far as possible, to become aware of it.

There will be three moments. Becoming aware (1) of our human and corporeal being, here and now; (2) of the mortality of our being; (3) of our being that is risen in Christ.

First of all, five minutes to recollect ourselves.

1. Now, stand up, feet slightly apart, arms dangling. Close your eyes. Allow the global sensation of your body to come, standing there, straight (not stiffly), poised flexibly on the axis of the vertebral column, itself sitting solidly on the pelvis.

Sway slightly to the right and to the left in order to feel the central axis better.

Take three complete breaths. Your whole attention follows the movement of the lungs and of the air. When exhaling, let the weight of your body flow downwards. Then allow the feeling of your head to come, of your shoulders, your right arm, your left arm, your right hand, your left hand, your back, your pelvis, your right leg, your left leg, of the slight ventral movement of your breathing, of the movement of your thorax, your mouth, your forehead, your eyes – of your global body.

Your consciousness is directly present in your bodily 'being-there' (do not imagine, or think, but feel that being-there); sway slightly on your feet, nearly imperceptibly, to maintain your suppleness. Feel the contact of your feet with the ground. You are a tree rooted in the earth, drawing its substance from the earth. Feel the sap rise through your feet, your legs, your spine, up to your head.

Allow the sensation of contact with your surroundings to come: the wind that caresses your face, the heat of the sun (if we are outside), the sounds that fall upon your ears. For a moment, open your eyes, welcome the light and what is before your eyes without looking for anything in detail. Then, close your eyes again.

Feel your body globally, and the movement of your breathing. You are, you are there, you are alive, rooted in the earth, conscious of the life you receive at every moment.

A few minutes of silence.

2.   Now, you are going to stretch out on the bare ground, on your back, your feet slightly apart, turned out, your arms stretched out along your body.

Abandon the weight of your body to the ground that supports it. Feel it pressed against the ground, as if it were going to enter into it. Take three full breaths. When exhaling let everything flow down.

Allow the feeling of your head to come, of your forehead, your mouth, the nape of your neck, your shoulders, your right shoulder, your left shoulder, your right arm, your left arm, your right hand, your left hand, your right shoulder blade, then your left, the right side of your torso, the left side, your right buttock, your left buttock, your right calf, your left calf, your right heel, your left heel, your whole right leg, your whole left leg, then the ventral movement of your breathing, the movement of your lower thorax, then your upper thorax, the air that passes through your nostrils.

Let the global sensation of your body come, stretched out there on the ground, and of the movement of your breathing.

A few moments for this awareness.

You are, you are there, you are mortal. This life that is given to you in the regular movement of your breathing will be withdrawn one day.

Let the sensation of that mortality, which is an essential dimension of your being, come. Feel the vulnerability of that faint breath, of your heart that beats, of your sentient body next to the hard ground.

Let the consciousness of all there is of death in you come:

our fears, our anguish, our intimate wounds, our flaws, our lies, our shame, our broken dreams, our secret pains, our defects, our sins, our guilt, the hardness of our heart that does not know how to love, the feeling of our death, the feeling of the ephemeral character of everything created that surrounds us, of our relationships with others, of nature, of matter itself.

Welcome that whole shadow element in ourselves; it is also us, a part of our truth, here and now, stretched out on the ground, on the earth from which we have come, to which we will return.

A few minutes' silence (at least five) in order to become aware of all this.

3.   Now, you are going to 'return', and gently you get up and sit down, either on the bare ground, or on something, in a circle, around this candle which I am going to light.

Let us look at the flame, quite simply, in silence, for a few moments. A flame that feeds on the substance of the wax and consumes it. A flame that is, however, of a different nature from the wax. Spirit.

Close your eyes for a moment, and try to interiorise this flame; repeat, opening and closing your eyes as often as necessary, until you see this flame interiorly, within your body, in your heart, shedding light, warmth and life there.

The Holy Spirit has been poured out into our heart, the prodigious gift of the divine life, a life which, in its flame, consumes our mortality and our weakness. It melts our heart of stone in order to transform it into a heart of flesh, a heart poor of self which has the radical power to love.

Let us enter into this luminous space in the depths of our heart, where the Spirit is, inexhaustible source of a life always new, of an absolutely new reality. Let us welcome that life, let us allow it to spread from the centre out to the periphery of our corporal being and of our actions.

That life is divine life, the life of Christ, communicated by the Spirit, making us enter into that movement of love and knowledge towards the Father which is our being as sons. The

ebb and flow of life, rhythm of all creation, image of the vital
rhythm of the Blessed Trinity, absolute gratuitousness of Love.

Let us surrender to that flame without fear the wax of our
mortal being. Let us have total confidence in him who is in us.
Let us abandon ourselves, body and soul, to the movement of
that life which, itself, is eternal. Let us allow ourselves to be
invaded by the gratuitousness of his joy, here and now.

A time of silence.

27

Paschal Joy

'Your pain will turn into joy . . .
and no one will take your joy from you.'

(John 16:20, 22)

We all want to have joy. Joy arises from the repose of the faculty
of desire in something that is good. The human will, by its very
nature, is orientated towards the good.

The whole of human wisdom is to know what is the true
good, for we can be mistaken. We can take wealth, power,
material or intellectual well-being, pleasure, even virtue, as the
object of our joy. The possession of these goods is the only
source of joy known to many of our contemporaries. But they
fall short of our potential. They are real goods, but not the
whole good.

And we who have given up marriage, the starting of a home
and family, and the free disposal of ourselves, are we con-
demned to a life of sadness, to a diminished life? That would
be a paradoxical result of a way of life which only makes sense
as an effort to live the Gospel fully, the Good News of our
peace and salvation.

The Gospel is a cause for joy. Mary was the first to celebrate it:

> 'My soul magnifies the Lord,
> and my spirit rejoices in God my Saviour.'
>
> (Luke 1:46–47)

The angel announces the birth of Christ in these terms:

> 'Do not be afraid; for see – I am bringing you good news
> of great joy for all the people.' (Luke 2:10)

The Gospel of Jesus is the proclamation of the Beatitudes. You poor, sinners, lowly ones, you are happy, for the Kingdom of God is yours. But the good he brings, the joy Jesus gives, these are different from the goods and joys that many people seek. Those who follow Christ can give up human joys without, for all that, being sad, for they possess a greater and infinitely more precious good. They are like the man who found a pearl of great price and who sold everything in order to have it.

Certainly, the wise of all ages have been able to rise above material goods and find their joy in virtue and wisdom. That is already a great deal. Others, of a more mystical inclination, have aspired to go beyond all created good in order to adhere to the Supreme Good; but that, for the majority, only expressed an inefficacious aspiration, for human beings by their own strength cannot give themselves eternal beatitude or its joy.

We are made for God. Our capacity for happiness is limitless – in that the philosophers were right, for no created good can fill it. That capacity is a capacity for personal knowledge and love, for union between persons, a union which can only be a free gift from one person to another. Hence grace. God has given us that grace in Christ. Christ is our joy. Joy had to come to meet us and take on a human face in order to fill our heart of flesh. For an abstract joy is not enough for us – we are human – but that face is unexpected and enigmatic.

PASCHAL JOY, THE JOY OF THE BEATITUDES

We are complex beings. We experience joy at many different levels according to the quality of the good we possess. There is a joy of the senses, a psychological joy, a spiritual joy (that is to say, a joy that is a fruit of the Holy Spirit in us). It is important to grasp that fact. It is possible for a deep, spiritual joy to coexist with the absence of sensed or psychological joys. At its ultimate limit, a limit that is observable in certain saints, suffering on the physical and emotional levels not only coexists with spiritual joy, but becomes itself, in a mysterious way, a source of joy. For example, St Thérèse of Lisieux: 'I have found happiness and joy on earth, but only in suffering.' Or again:

'The thought of heavenly happiness does not give me any joy, but still I ask myself at times how it will be possible to be happy without suffering. Jesus, no doubt, will change my nature. Otherwise I will miss suffering and the valley of tears.'

That is quite incomprehensible in a hedonist view of things that identifies pleasure, even if it is aesthetic and refined, with joy. Nor has it anything to do with a masochistic pleasure found in suffering. It only has meaning for the eyes of faith faced with beatifying realities which transcend the sensible and the human, and in the perspective of love which transforms everything it touches and consumes, our suffering just as well as our poor human joy.

At this moment, in England, a Carthusian brother not any older than myself is dying. There is no hope of recovery. He has only two or three months to live, or rather, to die slowly and in agony. And he is visibly radiant with joy.

Paschal joy is the joy of the Beatitudes, the joy of the poor in spirit, of the pure in heart, of those persecuted on account of Jesus (Matthew 5:10). It is not based on the possession of wealth, of talents, on success in this world, human love, repose or external tranquillity. It can even exist in the absence of all these things. It requires detachment from all that. It is founded on the unshakeable rock of Christ, of the love of God for us in Christ, on the eternal realities that we possess in faith and hope. We are loved by God. Already, we share in the divine life which will be our eternal bliss, our joy. No reality of this world, no sadness, no suffering can truly touch the source of our joy. Suffering and poverty only deepen further our capacity for true joy; they only remove the obstacles of our psychological short-sightedness. So one has some understanding of St Peter's extraordinary assertion – he who is also going to die on a cross.

> But rejoice in so far as you are sharing Christ's sufferings, so that you may also be glad and shout for joy when his glory is revealed. If you are reviled for the name of Christ, you are blessed, because the spirit of glory, which is the Spirit of God, is resting on you. (1 Peter 4:13–14)

The same Paschal alchemy which transforms suffering into

joy is to be seen at work in St Paul: 'I am now rejoicing in my sufferings for your sake' (Colossians 1:24).

It is not just any suffering that is a source of joy, but the sufferings of Christ in us: suffering endured for his name, through fidelity to him, in the service of the Church. And then it is not just any joy that is in us, but the joy of Christ, that joy which was in him on the night in which he was handed over to die, and which he communicated to his disciples, to his friends. So let us return to our text to see what that joy is.

The pains of giving birth

The context of our pericope is the announcement of Christ's departure. 'I am going to the Father' (John 16:18). But after a little while, the Lord will return: that is to say, he is going to die, but after three days God will raise him up and he will show himself to the disciples.

Christ contrasts the joy of the world in its apparent triumph with the sadness of the disciples thrown into despair. That pain is real. We need to see in it the solitude that follows separation from God, like that which will overwhelm Eve after the sin (Genesis 3:16ff). It will only disappear when the world is reconciled with its God. It is our pain also when we are far from God because of our sins, our infidelities, our selfish and small-minded preoccupations. Our solitude is painful in so far as we are separated from God.

But 'your pain will turn into joy' (John 16:20), because through the death of Christ the world will be reconciled with its Creator. In the glorified Christ God will be closer than ever. Suffering, in Christ, does not open onto nothingness. It is a giving birth, the birth of the new person, the passage from a mode of existence separated from God to a life of communion with him. The sadness of Christ works towards life, divine life – just like true solitude.

> 'When a woman is in labour, she has pain, because her hour has come. But when her child is born, she no longer remembers the anguish because of the joy of having brought a human being into the world.' (16:21)

That comparison was used by certain prophets to characterise the eschatological anguish of the end of the world (Isaiah 26:17; 66:7–14; Mark 13:8; Romans 8:22). With Christ's Resurrection the last times have come; in him the world has entered into its definitive state.

The image is very meaningful: the quality of suffering of a mother is very special. Does the mother ever completely lose sight of the new life, the new being, whose birth her pains precede? There are sufferings which are such only at a certain level; at a higher level, they are joy. The alchemy that effects the transmutation is love. And the transmutation is real. The saints do not play-act; they do not give the appearance of joy by an heroic act of the will. In all truth, in all simplicity, joy prevails over everything else in them, profound joy which radiates in their person.

However, there is an act of will which intervenes in it. In a very real sense one chooses to be joyful, but at a deeper level than that of feelings, at the level of the initial affirmation of the personality which expresses its will to be, its vital impetus. (The choice of the will which is part of the act of faith is situated at the same level.) It is not useless, therefore, to resolve to be joyful – it is even very important in determining the fundamental tonality of the person.

THE GRAIN OF WHEAT

Jesus gave another image of the fecundity of Paschal suffering: the grain of wheat, small, without beauty, unknown, hidden in the cold, dark earth. Dear grain of wheat, are you dead? If you have faith, if you can believe that God is able to draw the beauty and fecundity of life from your solitude – yes, I believe, for love is always fruitful. And even if my 'brother-grains' and I only see in each other the wrinkled husk, even if all we do is to rest alongside each other in the earth, one day we will gaze upon each other in the splendour of our beauty in the sun, on high, and we will rejoice in each other, and all together in the sun that gives us life.

'Very truly, I tell you, unless a grain of wheat falls into the earth and dies, it remains just a single grain; but if it dies, it bears much fruit.' (John 12:24)

That little image has always contributed more to my understanding of the fecundity of the hidden life than all learned books. Life is Paschal, at every level.

If for this life only we have hoped in Christ, we are of all people most to be pitied. But in fact Christ has been raised from the dead, the first fruits of those who have died. (1 Corinthians 15:19–20)

And such is the solidarity of the universe that it is not only the new humanity that is being born, but the new earth and also the new heavens.

For the creation waits with eager longing for the revealing of the children of God . . . We know that the whole creation has been groaning in labour pains until now . . . (Romans 8:19, 22)

Have you never felt that the hidden heart of the universe, of nature, beats in mysterious harmony with ours? It is not a question of a projection onto it of our inner feelings – though that also happens – but of a kinship of being and destiny. Sister earth, sister water!

CHRIST, OUR JOY

'So you have pain now; but I will see you again, and your hearts will rejoice, and no one will take your joy from you.' (John 16:22)

That happens to the letter. On the evening of Easter day the Lord appears to the disciples and 'the disciples rejoiced when they saw the Lord' (John 20:20). And no one will take that joy from them: the world or anything in the world cannot affect it, for Jesus has conquered the world (John 16:33). His joy comes from elsewhere. It is eschatological joy, joy of the world of the

Resurrection, beyond the tribulations of this world and beyond death. It is eternal, like the life of the glorified Christ.

The joy of the Christian is a grace. We enter into the joy of our Master (Matthew 25:21) as one enters into the warmth of a brightly lit fireside – as into the arms of someone we love. Christ communicates his own joy to us, the joy of his heart which sees the Father face to face, which always does the Father's will, which has received the anointing of the Spirit of love. 'I have said these things to you so that my joy may be in you, and that your joy may be complete' (John 15:11). His joy is the sap of life that passes through the vine and runs into the branches, making them abundantly fruitful (John 15:5).

'I will see you again, and your hearts will rejoice.' Our joy is born of a personal encounter with Christ in faith and love. He comes into our heart according to his promise, like a mysterious guest, at the invitation of our faith and our fidelity to his commandments. It is not a question of an airy-fairy emotion, but of a union founded solidly on the conformity of our will with his and an effective love.

> 'They who have my commandments and keep them are those who love me; and those who love me will be loved by my Father, and I will love them and reveal myself to them.' (John 14:21)

> 'We will come to them and make our home with them.' (John 14:23)

No one will take that joy from us

There is our joy! It is fellowship with the Father and with his Son Jesus Christ (1 John 1:3) in the Spirit of truth who also 'abides with you, and will be in you' (John 14:17). It is not something transitory, subject to the fickleness of our emotions. It 'abides' in us, constant and solid, deeper than our griefs or elations. It is love and knowledge, divine life, the life of the glorified Christ in us. Just as he 'became for us wisdom from God, and righteousness and sanctification and redemption' (1 Corinthians 1:30), Christ also became our joy. No one will take that joy from us. No one can wrest us from Jesus' heart.

Who will separate us from the love of Christ? Will hardship, or distress, or persecution, or famine, or nakedness, or peril, or sword? . . . No, in all these things we are more than conquerors through him who loved us. For I am convinced that neither death, nor life, nor angels, nor rulers, nor things present, nor things to come, nor powers, nor height, nor depth, nor anything else in all creation, will be able to separate us from the love of God in Christ Jesus our Lord. (Romans 8:35, 37–39)

Love and joy, it is all one. The joy of God is his love. Our joy is his love poured into our heart (Romans 5:5), it is Christ in us.

Let us not forget that Christ, the King of glory, is in us as our friend, with all that that implies by way of intimacy, exchange of knowledge and love, equality (it must be said, the grace of Christ goes that far), sharing of everything, good and bad, identity of destiny. Think how we would prize the intimate friendship of a noble, great, beautiful person! What a light it would shed on our whole life! How, for a man, the love of a beautiful woman with a deep, limpid soul, changes and enhances his whole life! But here, the One who calls himself our friend is the Lord. He does not lie. He does not speak empty words. He has paid dearly for the right to be our friend. He has proved himself to be such.

'No one has greater love than this, to lay down one's life for one's friends. You are my friends if you do what I command you. I do not call you servants any longer, because the servant does not know what the master is doing; but I have called you friends, because I have made known to you everything that I have heard from my Father. You did not choose me but I chose you.' (John 15:13–16)

Christ, the Word of God, absolute Truth, addresses these words to us. How could we not always have a source of joy in the depths of our heart, even at times when all sensible joy eludes us? How could we not feel the need to communicate with Jesus in the intimacy of our heart? Isn't that what makes solitude sweet? 'Rejoice in the Lord always; again I will say, Rejoice' (Philippians 4:4) – *always*, because the love of Christ envelops us always.

Joy and prayer

The communion between Christ and us is such that we see everything with his eyes, and in him we are introduced into the Father's intimacy, to the extent that 'if you ask anything of the Father in my name, he will give it to you' (16:23). We address our prayer directly to the Father, and the Father gives because of the Son. Our prayer is heard because of our union with Christ; it is heard because it is Christ's prayer in us. I live, I love, I pray – no, not I, it is Christ who lives, loves, prays in me.

Christ exhorts us to pray: 'Ask and you will receive, so that your joy may be complete' (16:24). Our joy comes from God, we must humbly ask him for it. And it will be consummated in the prayer of intimate union with Christ.

Joy and communion

When I say that Christ is our joy, I mean to speak of the total Christ. For our joy is realised not only in our communion with Jesus, but also in our communion with those we love in him, with those who are his members. The joy of the love of a dear one, the joy of loving him in Christ, that is the pure joy of the Spirit in us. It can even be that this joy has stronger resonances in our senses than our love for God. That does not matter, for it can only exist in that love. Let us accept that joy, therefore, openly and gently from the hands of Christ.

By its very nature, joy communicates itself, just as light shines and heat warms. It cannot remain enclosed in the heart. It wants to give itself to others. The joy of the first Christians expressed itself in the sharing of everything, in brotherly fellowship, the Eucharist and prayer in common, in cheerfulness and simplicity of heart (Acts 2:42–47). St Paul exhorts those who exercise compassion towards their brothers, to do so 'in cheerfulness' (Romans 12:8).

To show joy in our relationship with others is the supreme

delicacy of genuine love. Sadness is nearly always selfish. Joy is the courage of faith, the vitality of love.

Hidden joy

However, our joy is refracted through the temperament of each one. There are those who express it with naturalness and ease. Others only succeed with much difficulty in showing something of an interior that is rich nevertheless. Still others are subject to sudden fluctuations between joy and sadness, at least on the psychological level. Others are of an easily melancholic disposition. Temperament, education, personal history – all that marks our joy. Faith and grace take us as we are and espouse our natural make-up – at least in the short term, for with time, the profound realities of our life in Christ, the patient work of the Spirit, should rectify our faults, while allowing us to be ourselves, or, to speak more correctly, while permitting us to be our true selves.

Sometimes, sadness veils the substantial joy in us. We must not, above all, be despondent because of that: that would be to compound the harm. Christ was sorrowful even to death in the garden of Gethsemane. At these moments, our joy is a joy of pure faith. We believe in Love, in the substantial Joy in us, and we walk in that light as if we could see. Let us humbly admit our weakness and let us pray to the Spirit to give us joy, the joy of Christ in our human heart, in so far as that would serve the glory of God.

Let each one try to become more transparent to the joy of the Spirit. Above all, let us not be ashamed to be joyful, to be cheerful. Let us not purchase the more than questionable name of being 'a serious man' at the cost of a sullen face. That is not the Spirit of charity.

If you sparkle like champagne, be our festive wine. If your make-up is rather that of limpid, tranquil water, be our joy in repose. If you are a deep, red wine which takes on the colour of fire in the sun, be our joy which is able to assume and transform suffering and absence. Let each one be a presence of Christ's joy among us: cheerful or quiet, radiant or discreetly smiling, it matters little. It is indeed the tradition of St Bruno:

'*Esse suos laetos, laetus et ipse cupit*' (Posthumous Praise no. 149 from Ponlevoy): 'A joyful man, he loved to see his own joyful'. '*Semper erat festo vulto . . .*' (Posthumous Praise from Calabria): 'He always had a joyful face'.

Fruit of the Spirit

It is clear that the joy of which we speak is not a joy measured by the personal satisfactions that life offers us. The joy of Christ in us can only be the fruit of the action of the Spirit in our hearts.

> The fruit of the Spirit is love, joy, peace, patience, kindness, generosity, faithfulness, gentleness and self-control.
> (Galatians 5:22–23)

There where the Spirit is, there is joy. We make fun of the naïve and perhaps slightly hysterical demonstrations of certain modern Pentecostalists. Certainly, they sometimes place the joy of the Spirit at a level that is too superficial. However, we feel in some obscure way that if we were truly open to the Spirit whose presence in us we do not doubt, if we could give ourselves to God like children, without inhibitions, without restrictions, with all our heart, then a joy which surpasses all joy would rise up in us, the joy of Love.

> Be glad and rejoice for ever
>   in what I am creating;
> for I am about to create Jerusalem as a joy,
>   and its people as a delight.
> I will rejoice in Jerusalem,
>   and delight in my people.
>   (Oracle of the Lord, Isaiah 65:18)

> That we may be received with you into the glory of the
>   Father,
> Come, Lord Jesus.

> That with your glory we may be glorified,
> Come, Lord Jesus.

That you may be our joy which no one can take from us,
Come, Lord Jesus.

(The intercessory prayers of Eastertide)

28

The Good Shepherd

'For the Lamb at the centre of the throne will be
their shepherd,
    and he will guide them to springs of the water of
life.'

(Revelation 7:17)

There is no image of the Saviour as exploited by Christian art
as that of the Good Shepherd. However, it too often puts before
us an idyllic, somewhat effeminate figure, with insipid colours
– in short, something very different from the rough, nomadic
shepherd who inspired the words of Christ and who, alone,
faces the wild beasts and the harshness of the climate. For the
Christians of the first centuries, the image of the shepherd
summed up the whole work of salvation, it embellished all the
catacombs, at that epoch it was what the image of the Crucified
is for the faithful of our days.

However, in our urbanised culture, the words 'shepherd',
'sheep' and 'flock' have ended up having a pejorative meaning
when they are applied to people. I had, for a few months, a
Father Master who used to speak of us, his novices, as his
sheep. That used to make me furious! I was a comical sheep
besides, at thirty years of age, used to managing alone in the
tough world of men since the death of my father which happened when I was fourteen.

In its pejorative acceptation, the term 'sheep' immediately
evokes the absence of personality and character, subjection and
passivity. The word 'flock' makes one think spontaneously of
a gregarious, impersonal and even depersonalising gathering,
levelled down, without initiative and without variety, shut into
rigid frameworks or structures – in a word, a spineless mass.

'Shepherd' in that context can only mean 'dictator' or 'guard-dog'.

So we should indeed make a conscious effort to go beyond the stereotype, in order to grasp the profound reality that those words wish to reveal to us. First, let us look at the Gospel of the Sunday, John 10:11–18, or better, the whole tenth chapter. Let us go to the essential content of the chapter: Christ defines himself as shepherd: 'I am the good shepherd.' He does not speak of good shepherds, in general. He only speaks of himself, the One who meets us here and now, the Lord, whether we know him or not, who is in the midst of our life and of the life of the Church and of humanity, as the one who goes and calls, gathers, directs, enlightens and consoles. Christ makes his own the message of the Old Testament's 'shepherd of Israel', that is to say, of God himself (cf. Psalm 23, Psalm 80, Isaiah 40:11 and, above all, Ezekiel 34).

So, for his audience it is a known image. 'I myself will be the shepherd of my sheep, and I will make them lie down, says the Lord God' (Ezekiel 34:15). Like all the Johannine passages with '*ego eimi*', 'I am', Jesus presents himself in chapter 10 as the Lord in history. 'I am the good shepherd' has here the value of a solemn, theophanic discourse. The shepherd, Christ, is the one to whom the Father has confided those who are his. 'They were yours,' says Christ in the sacerdotal prayer in John 17, 'you gave them to me' (John 17:6). (This whole magnificent prayer is the transposition into other terms of the parable of the shepherd.) He received his role from the Father, he expresses his obedience to the Father who sent him and he manifests before humankind the love of the Father.

By proclaiming himself the Good Shepherd, Jesus professes that he assumes without reserve the responsibility for those who are entrusted to him. Always new, this proclamation assures us of the unfailing presence of the Saviour. He is the Good Shepherd. Let us read this Gospel as his word addressed, here and now, to us.

'I KNOW MY OWN AND MY OWN KNOW ME' (10:14)

The bond that unites Christ and us is not only a function assumed by obedience, an external bond, but more profoundly, a bond of mutual knowledge and love. It rests on a community of life and a solidarity of interest between him and us. It is intimate presence to one another, reciprocal understanding and trust. We know his voice, our heart knows how to recognise it. We follow him where he leads us. And Jesus knows us, he calls, not in a general, anonymous way, but he calls each one of us by name. That is true of each Christian, for the relationship with Christ is always a person-to-person relationship, but there is tangible evidence of it in the extremely personal form the monastic vocation – and especially the solitary vocation – takes in each case. These vocations are clearly individualised: 'To the praise of the glory of God, Christ, the Father's Word, has through the Holy Spirit, from the beginning chosen certain men, whom he willed to lead into solitude and unite to himself in intimate love', say the first words of our Statutes. 'And he leads them out' (John 10:3). The call of Christ demands a rupture, a departure from the domain of the known towards the unknown, in the footsteps of Christ.

'I know mine and mine know me,' says Christ, 'just as the Father knows me and I know the Father' (John 10:15). Now the intimacy between the Father and the Son is a presence of the one in the other: 'The Father is in me and I am in the Father' (John 10:38). Besides, where there is love, there is reciprocal presence. Such is the mutual relationship between Christ and us: 'On that day you will know that I am in my Father, and you in me, and I in you' (John 14:20).

There is more than an analogy between this intimacy and that which unites the Father and the Son; the reciprocal knowledge and love of the Father and the Son are the very source of the reciprocal knowledge and love of Jesus and his own; there is participation of the one in the other, a broadening, an expansion of the one to become the other, like a luminous heat that spreads.

This human participation in the divine intimacy is eternal

life itself. Jesus came so that humankind might have that life 'and that they may have it abundantly' (10:10). These are the pastures that he opens up before us, inexhaustible pastures.

THE SACRIFICE OF THE SHEPHERD

But the road to life goes through Calvary. 'The good shepherd lays down his life for his sheep.' He gives it freely. No one takes it from him (10:18). Christ is recognisable by this trait. He manifests by the gift of his life the infinite earnestness of his love, the absolute unselfishness with which he took charge of us. He does not flee, like the mercenary, before the danger that threatens us. The mercenary only loves himself and he saves himself. Faced with the enemy, Christ exposes himself to death. Here the metaphor bursts under the weight of the reality, and the image of the shepherd merges with that of the lamb, the slain Lamb who will be the shepherd of the redeemed in heaven (Revelation 7:17). In the person of the shepherd the redemptive figure of the suffering Servant of Isaiah 53 is fulfilled.

The role of Christ the Shepherd does not end on the tragic note of his death. If he lays down his life, it is in order to take it up again (10:17). He is the master of it. His sacrifice is desired only with a view to his resurrection. Through that he brings the work of our salvation to its completion, he guides us to 'springs of the water of life' (Revelation 7:17), up to the gift of eternal life and of the Spirit who will realise in us the intimate life of God.

That is the ultimate end. But already we are raised to life in Christ, already we have received the guarantee of the Spirit, already the love of God has been poured out into our hearts. Can we not hope, ask Christ to lead us 'to the springs of the water of life' which are the beginning of the realisation of that life of intimacy with God in our hearts, in prayer and love?

Come, Holy Spirit! Fill the hearts of your faithful!
And enkindle in them the fire of your love! Alleluia!

ONE SHEPHERD ONLY

The mission of the Good Shepherd is universal: his role is to bring about the unity of all by uniting them in a personal union with himself, to 'gather into one the dispersed children of God' (John 11:52). Jesus does not speak of leading those he calls to the fold of the Old Covenant, but of incorporating them into the one flock of those he guides to eternal life. 'I have other sheep that do not belong to this fold. I must bring them also, and they will listen to my voice. So there will be one flock, one shepherd' (John 10:16). Note that Christ says 'one flock' and not 'one sheepfold' or fold, as the Vulgate translates it (*'fiet unum ovile'*). The unity of the Church does not come about by attachment to a place or an external structure, but to a person; it is the person of Jesus Christ who unites his own. One understands the ecumenical import of this parable. Christ's arms embrace all without distinction of race, nation or even religion. 'Holy Father . . . that they may be one, as we are one' (John 17:11). 'In that renewal there is no longer Greek and Jew, circumcised and uncircumcised, barbarian, Scythian, slave and free; but Christ is all and in all!' (Colossians 3:11).

THE HUMAN SHEPHERDS

When we say that the bishops and priests are shepherds, we cannot forget that Scripture applies this word first of all to God and to Christ, and in a sense that can never be true of anyone else whomsoever. God alone is the supreme Shepherd, whose face is visibly reflected in him who is his image, Christ, the Good Shepherd. The Church is the body of Christ, whose members, 'although watched over by human shepherds . . . are nevertheless ceaselessly led and brought to pasture by Christ himself, the Good Shepherd and the prince of shepherds', Vatican 2, the pastoral Council par excellence, assures us.

Sacraments of Christ

The Church belongs only to Christ. The human shepherds are not shepherds on their own account. They do not replace a

neglectful, drunken or inadequate Shepherd. They are rather –
and it is their whole dignity – the 'sacraments' (taking the word
here in a broad sense) of the Good Shepherd, those who at one
and the same time render him present in the capacity of
Shepherd and are the servants of his permanent activity for the
good of the Church. They are those who act '*in persona Christi*',
through whom Christ acts. They fulfil their role to the extent
of their being transparent to Christ, and of their docility to the
action of his Spirit.

Their activity will necessarily have the same purpose as that
of the Good Shepherd: the gathering, the unity, the communion of all people with God and among themselves. The
Church's work is a work of unity. The whole Church, and each
one of its members, throughout their life and by their love
participate in it. But within the Church, the human shepherds
are the 'sacraments' of the Good Shepherd in his activity as
leader uniting people. The shepherd's role, therefore, is to
create unity. They are true shepherds to the extent that they
work for unity, not focused on themselves, but on Christ, of
whom they are the visible presence and the servants.

They render Christ present in the proclamation of the Word
of God in all its forms, in the celebration of the sacraments
and in the government of the people of God, where it is a
question above all of spiritual authority to build up the Church
and form the image of Christ in souls. Their perspectives are
those of Christ: not only the members of the Catholic Church,
but all people are the object of their ministry – according to
each one's vocation, of course. Contemplatives, in so far as
their activity does not pass through created means and does
not suffer their limitations in time and space, should above all
make their own this universal open-mindedness and concern.
Situated in the depths of the heart of the Church, by their love
they should reach all the members of the Body, that is to say,
all humanity.

Other Christs

The human shepherd should be an 'other Christ'. He should bear his mark. He should be able to say, like Paul, 'Be imitators of me, as I am of Christ.'

> Tend the flock of God that is in your charge . . . not under compulsion but willingly, as God would have you do it – not for sordid gain but eagerly. Do not lord it over those in your charge, but be examples to the flock. (1 Peter 5:2–3)

The human shepherd has his special role within the Church, but that does not put him above or outside others; on the contrary, that obliges him in a new way to be a member of the Church, with the requirement to be more faithful, more submissive and more like the prince of shepherds, Christ. His first duty is to be and to live what he has the responsibility of proposing to others and having them live. Following the example of Christ who was at one and the same time Shepherd and Lamb, Shepherd because he was Lamb, giving himself for the life of his own, the human shepherd is also sent to be the servant of all.

To be a shepherd is not first of all an honour or an authority, but a responsibility in the strong sense of the word, in the sense in which Jesus Christ was responsible for each and every one by bearing their miseries and their sins, as well as their riches and their joys.

> 'Whoever wishes to be first among you must be slave of all. For the Son of Man came not to be served but to serve, and to give his life a ransom for many.' (Mark 10:44–45)

Service of charity

The function of the shepherd is to preside, but the presidency in question is that of unity and charity, and it will be realised by sacrifice and service. He presides in Christ's place as the servant of that unity which comes about in charity. His service is directed towards living people in view of their communion in God. It should be based on a mutual knowledge and love, the fabric of human, heartfelt bonds. The soul of the pastoral attitude can only be charity. 'Simon, do you love me more than these? . . . feed my lambs, feed my sheep' (John 21:15–17). One is a shepherd to the extent of one's love for Christ and for others. The Church is built on love or it does not exist. The spiritual authority that the human shepherd receives from Christ is not his own property. It has to be stripped of all arrogance, of all arbitrariness, of all human interest, of all power-seeking, all desire to use it for oneself. It must be borne in humility and poverty.

That authority is not meant to subjugate but to liberate, to free. The shepherd does not take the place of people, even before God. He works to promote their liberty to adhere freely to Christ. The Church is not a flock in the bad sense of the word, a mass surrendered into the hands of some leader or other. It is a community of persons. God, by his grace, creates freedom. The Good Shepherd came to make people free. The shepherds are at the service of that spiritual liberation. They must be attentive to the Spirit in those in their care, for the freedom in question is the freedom of the Spirit of God, not human arbitrariness.

Through that pastoral charity the shepherd is called to sanctify himself, to resemble the Good Shepherd by dying to himself and living for God.

THE ROLE OF THE SHEPHERDS IN THE CHARTERHOUSE

The word 'shepherd' does not figure in our Statutes, but its reality is to be seen in the Prior and in those to whom his authority is delegated: the Procurator for the Brothers, the Father Master for the novices, the confessors, the Vicar, etc.

The Prior
The same evangelical qualities which we have just indicated are met again. It is striking, in fact, that the Statutes insist on the unifying role of the Prior, and that not focused on himself but 'in Christ' (3.6). He is present among his brothers as the one

who serves 'after the example of Christ' and who gives the example of what he proposes to others (33.6). Concern, humility, cordiality, firmness, adaptability to persons, respect and promotion of their responsible freedom, unselfishness, etc. – such are the qualities required of the Prior (ch. 21). The Statutes give as the foundation of the attitude of obedience, the fact that the Prior represents God (10.13); to refuse to obey him is in reality 'resisting not him but God, whose place he holds in our regard' (7.8). In short, the Prior assures a certain presence of Christ, the supreme Shepherd, in our house, and he will do that all the more effectively the more he is conformed to Christ in his person and docile to the Spirit of Christ in his actions and words. The paternal and fraternal authority ('*primus inter pares*') that is granted to him establishes him as servant of his brothers, and his service is a service of charity and unity.

The Master of novices

To the Master of novices is confided the formation of the novices, to whom he must provide monastic and Carthusian instruction, moral formation, spiritual direction and appropriate help in time of trial (9.4). He must develop in them love for Christ and for the Church, a deep spirit of prayer and of intimate union with God (9.5). He must progressively form them in the responsible exercise of their freedom, 'to the holy liberty of our vocation' to solitude, say the Statutes (9.7). One can say that all his authority is at the service of the liberty of the novices, for the goal of formation is to establish them in a kind of continual progression in divine intimacy; this is an exchange of love and knowledge within a personal and reciprocal relationship which only has meaning and cannot exist except in the spontaneity of the heart in liberty (9.5: 1.4). The activity of the Father Master must progressively disappear before that of the Spirit of Christ in the heart of the novice, whom he will have trained in the discernment of spirits. In this sense, the Father Master's role is more that of a 'servant', more humble yet than that of the Prior.

All sorts of qualities are also asked of the Father Master: judgement, maturity, charity, observance, love of vocation, a

contemplative and peaceful spirit, open-mindedness, adaptability, understanding (9.1), a maternal heart and the vigour of
a father. Just that! He receives his authority from the Prior and
must collaborate with him in the exercise of his office, while
having the necessary autonomy in the formation of the novices.

I will limit myself to these two shepherds. You will find the
same characteristics for the others who have care of souls in
the house. But I ask one thing of you: when you read all the
qualities that the Statutes require of superiors, do not be scandalised not to find them in them. The Statutes propose an
ideal, the superiors realise it according to what is possible for
them. One has such a fault, the other has another. Every one
has his limitations, all one can ask of them is that the results
of the exercise of their office be rather positive on the whole,
and that they endeavour to attain the ideal with perseverance
and humility. And do not look at things from the outside.
Maybe, one day, you will have to take upon you the service of
your brothers, and it is not certain that you will not find limitations and defects in yourselves. We are men. Let us accept
one another as men. Let us gladly help those who have the
responsibility of serving us, through an intelligent co-operation.
And let us always think that it is Christ who works through
them, and that he knows how to write straight with crooked
lines.

It is, perhaps, the mark of our solitary vocation that, with
us, the role of shepherds, although very important, should
nevertheless remain modest and discreet, more self-effacing
before the supreme Shepherd than elsewhere. For, in the final
analysis, only the Spirit of Christ can lead to the living waters
of love and contemplation.

29

The Going of Christ, the Coming of the Spirit

'It is to your advantage that I go away, for if I do not go away, the Advocate will not come to you; but if I go, I will send him to you.'

(John 16:7)

From the fifth Sunday of Easter onwards, the Liturgy turns our attention distinctly towards the coming of the Spirit, who alone can realise the mystery of Christ in our inner being. Here we find once more, as in the second week, the need to go beyond sensible experience in order to have access to a deeper relationship with Christ. There, it was considered from the perspective of a purified faith; here, it is considered in its connection with the gift of the Holy Spirit. The absence of Christ is revealed as a mystery of presence.

'If I do not go away, the Advocate will not come to you.' 'Go away' – what does that mean? For the man Jesus it is a question of leaving this earth and returning to the Father. That is not a mere change of location. Through the images of space and place, it is the glorification of Christ, realised by his death, resurrection and ascension, that is in question; or from St John's perspective – for he does not speak explicitly of the Ascension – it is the return into the presence of the Father in the one upward movement by which Christ was 'raised up' on the Cross in order to enter into the glory of the Father who raised him from the dead. The Easter apparitions were only an interlude necessary for laying the foundations for faith and the Church's witness. They had to end quickly, to make way for the economy of the presence of Christ in the Spirit.

THE BODY OF CHRIST, SOURCE OF THE SPIRIT

Why is the gift of the Spirit subject to Jesus' return into the Father's presence? Jesus revealed the reason for it a long time beforehand, during his public ministry, at the festival of Tabernacles. The deliverance from Egypt and the wandering life in the desert were being celebrated. On the final day, they celebrated in a special way the waters that gushed forth from the rock in the desert, symbol of the Messianic waters of salvation which the prophets had foretold for the future.

'With joy you will draw water from the wells of salvation,' said Isaiah (12:3), and again:

> They did not thirst when he led them through the deserts;
> he made water flow for them from the rock;
> he split open the rock and the water gushed out.
>
> (Isaiah 48:21)

At the high point of the Liturgy, while a priest was bringing in water amidst 'Hosannas' and the rustling of palms, a man began to proclaim in a loud voice:

> 'Let anyone who is thirsty come to me, and let the one who believes in me drink. As the scripture has said, "Out of the believer's heart shall flow rivers of living water."'
> (John 7:37–38)

That man was Jesus.

St John explains the meaning of that proclamation to us: the water Jesus was speaking about was the Spirit. 'Now he said this about the Spirit, which believers in him were to receive.' But later on. For, as yet 'there was no Spirit, because Jesus was not yet glorified' (John 7:39). Only the glorified Christ dispenses the Spirit. The bodily humanity of Christ is the source of the Spirit, it is the spiritual rock of the desert (1 Corinthians 10:4), but it must be struck with the rod of the Cross, so that the rivers of living water may gush forth from it (Origen). St John, and the Fathers after him, saw the symbolic realisation of that promise in the flow of blood and water from the pierced body of Christ on the Cross (John 19:34). The water symbolises the Spirit; the blood, the humanity of Christ which bleeds in the Passion. Through the blood poured out, we receive the Spirit.

Note well the realistic idea of St John. He places the source of the Spirit, 'spiritual' reality par excellence, in the *body* of Christ. But that cannot come about without a radical transformation of Christ's humanity: unless, according to the terminology of St Paul, the last Adam becomes 'a life-giving spirit' (1 Corinthians 15:45).

So that the man Jesus can give us the Spirit and thus bring us into the Kingdom of God, he must return to the Father. The Father has to give him that divine glory he had in the presence of the Father before the world existed (John 17:5). His humanity must be transformed by the divine light of the Word, embraced by the flame of the Spirit, must become 'spiritual' to the point of becoming the source of the Holy Spirit for those who touch it through faith and the sacraments.

For Christ's flesh is not replaced by a purely spiritual presence of God. It remains the point of contact; the Incarnation remains for ever. Only its way of being present and acting is more universal and more interior; the sensible presence is effected through the sacraments of the faith, by which the glorified Christ touches us and infuses the Spirit into our hearts. Think of that sometimes at the moment of Communion during Mass; at that moment, our lips press against the open side of the Crucified and we drink deep of incorruptible Love. 'Those who eat my flesh and drink my blood have eternal life' (John 6:54).

The necessary separation
The need for separation from Jesus can be definitely seen, on the human level, in the behaviour of the disciples. They loved Christ, no one can doubt that, but with a human, fragile love still. They had no access to the innermost heart of Christ's divine personality. Their understanding was not equal to their heart, nor their heart at the level of the Spirit.

'Where I am going, you cannot follow me now; but you will follow afterwards,' says Jesus. Indignant, the ardent Peter protests his love unto death. 'Lord, why can I not follow you now? I will lay down my life for you.' Presumption, Peter! 'The spirit indeed is willing, but the flesh is weak' (Mark 14:38). 'Will you lay down your life for me? Very truly, I tell you, before the cock crows, you will have denied me three times' (John 13:36–38). Which of us has not the impression sometimes that those words are addressed to him?

One senses the lucid and affectionate sympathy in Jesus' eyes as he looks at the disciples, the magnitude of the events being so far beyond them. 'I still have many things to say to you, but you cannot bear them now' (John 16:12). Let us grasp once and for all the radical insufficiency of the flesh, of the human left to its own resources, in the things of God. We must bring to it our good will and our enthusiasm, but let us be well aware that those do not go very far; they are not equal to the task. That does not mean that we should be purely passive. 'The one who believes in me will also do the works that I do and, in fact, will do greater works than these, because I am going to the Father' (John 14:12), says the Lord, 'and from the Father's heart I will send you the Spirit' (cf. 14:16). Our co-operation with grace is necessary, and will take the form of an effective love, but that will be a fruit of the Spirit in us, it will have its source in the power and love of God and not in our human strength.

At times, in his mercy, God allows us to experience this insufficiency, but not in order to crush us. If, of ourselves, we can do nothing (John 15:5), in Christ, by the power of his Spirit, we can do all things.

> In any and all circumstances I have learned the secret of being well-fed and of going hungry, of having plenty and of being in need. I can do all things through him who strengthens me. (Philippians 4:12–13)

True evangelical poverty is situated beyond the wealth and poverty of this world. It is total freedom and trust, founded on the unconditional surrender of ourselves into the Father's hands. The most tremendous audacity is allowed it, is even normal for it. It is as if a tiny hand-held dynamo were taken from us, in order to plug us into a power-station of unlimited capacity – and it is prayer made in the confidence of faith that opens the way to the divine energy.

> To him who by the power at work within us is able to accomplish abundantly far more than all we can ask or imagine, to him be glory in the church and in Christ Jesus to all generations, for ever and ever. Amen. (Ephesians 3:20–21)

Presence in absence

So we understand that Christ can present his departure as something which is to our advantage. But if he goes away, he will return. His absence is but the condition for his presence. We must not imagine the presence of Jesus and the presence of the Spirit as two presences which succeed each other in time. On the contrary, the gift of the Spirit is also Christ's presence in us, a more intimate and efficacious presence, a presence of love.

> 'You heard me say to you, "I am going away, and I am coming to you." If you loved me, you would rejoice that I am going to the Father, because the Father is greater than I.' (John 14:28)

It is true. Our love is feeble and selfish. We think only of ourselves. If we love Christ – how that 'if' hurts! – we must rejoice that he is going to the Father, for he says, 'the Father is greater than I'. It is not a question here of an essential subordination of the Son to the Father, but of the Son's state of humiliation, voluntarily assumed, which the Father will respond to by glorifying him. We see that for Christ, to go to the Father is an object of joy and desire, for it is the full flowering of the Father's victorious love in him, and through and in him, in us and in the whole universe.

THE PARACLETE

Who is the Paraclete whom Jesus promises? The exact sense of the word 'Paraclete' is one of those most debated. In itself, this

Greek word belongs to legal vocabulary and means: 'he who is called to assist', the 'advocate', the counsel for the defence. From there, we see the meaning 'consoler', or 'intercessor', appear. The expression which in the New Testament appears only in the work of John, designates at one time the Spirit, at another time Christ (1 John 2:1). The diverse nuances indicated above are more or less present, the emphasis resting on one or the other according to the individual case. The best indication of the precise sense meant in each case will be the function that is attributed to the Paraclete.

The Advocate (John 16:8–11)

The Paraclete appears first of all in the role of advocate, in a process whose protagonists are Jesus and the world. That process is present right through St John's Gospel. The world, represented by the Jews, refuses, judges and condemns Jesus. But another judgement happens in the believer's heart in the light of the Spirit whom the world does not know. The one who is judged becomes the judge. The proceedings are initiated on the subject of the nature of sin, the nature of justice, the nature of judgement. Each time, the Spirit confounds the world.

- Its sin consists in its refusal to believe in Jesus, in its refusal of the light.

- Justice, throughout the proceedings, is what is accorded to the advantage of the litigant who is in the right. That justice was accorded to Christ in the act by which the Father called him back to himself by bringing him back to life and exalting him, so that the disciples did not see him any more after the Easter apparitions.

- The judgement of condemnation of the one who ruled the world is necessarily implied, and is already pronounced in Christ's victory.

So, thanks to the Spirit, and contrary to all appearances, a conviction grows in our hearts: it is not the world, it is Jesus who is right; so, we too are right to believe, we are right to dedicate ourselves to Christ's cause; in him, we are already conquerors of the world and of the devil.

This function of the Spirit remains relevant today, for the process with the world still continues, and we need our Advocate to convince it of its mistake, for the world still believes itself to be right in its opposition to Christ. Monastic life can be regarded as raised up by the Spirit as a testimony of faith in Christ's victory and in the risen life.

The Spirit of truth
'When the Spirit of truth comes, he will guide you into all the truth' (John 16:13). The Paraclete is called the Spirit of Truth because he is the Spirit of Christ, who, himself, is the Truth. Certainly, Christ revealed everything, he opened his heart to his disciples: 'I have made known to you everything that I have heard from my Father' (John 15:15). But they are unable to understand, to 'bear' it, says the Gospel, employing a word used most often in the context of the Passion (19:17). Why are they unable to understand? Are they not intelligent enough or sufficiently cultured? No, for the wise of this world did not recognise the wisdom of God revealed in the Cross of Jesus; to human intelligence, it is foolishness (1 Corinthians 1:18–31). 'I thank you, Father, Lord of heaven and earth, because you have hidden these things from the wise and the intelligent and have revealed them to infants' (Matthew 11:25).

The wisdom of God so transcends what we can imagine, that it can only be received by the humble in spirit who open themselves in total simplicity to the divine light, that is to say, to the light brought by Christ.

> 'All things have been handed over to me by my Father; and no one knows the Son except the Father, and no one knows the Father except the Son and anyone to whom the Son chooses to reveal him.' (Matthew 11:27)

The truth that Jesus reveals is the manifestation of the intimate life of God, a participation in the knowledge of the Father. It is not an 'objective' truth which remains outside us, like a scientific datum about material realities, but a reciprocal knowledge between persons which demands an intimate and transforming encounter. This knowledge is only realised in love, the gift of oneself. But the depth of contact is determined by what we are, and what we are is infinitely below what God is. That is why the disciples are unable to bear that truth. They are not equal to it. We are not equal to it. That truth demands too much of us: a participation in a mystery that frightens and disorientates us. Our heart is too small. We do not understand, because we do not want to understand, because we do not love enough.

God has to transform us, has to give us a principle of knowledge and love that would be at his level. But there is none, except his own knowledge and his own love, his Word and his Spirit. The Word of God has revealed him in the objectivity of a human nature and a human life. That was only for a short period of time. It will be up to the Spirit who dwells in our hearts to introduce us from within into that knowledge, and to enable us to live according to the mind of God and the spirit of Christ.

The thoughts of God 'no one comprehends . . . except the Spirit of God', he who 'searches everything, even the depths of God'. And it is that Spirit that we have received, 'the Spirit that is from God, so that we may understand the gifts bestowed on us by God' (1 Corinthians 2:12). 'We have the mind of Christ' (1 Corinthians 2:16) says St Paul, as if it were the equivalent of having the Spirit of God.

Spirit of love

We know that in the divine life it is from the reciprocal love of the Father and the Son that the Spirit proceeds. We readily call him the Spirit of love. It is he who pours out the love of God in our hearts (Romans 5:5). How is he also the principle of light, of truth? Precisely because he is Love. By giving us the Spirit, the Father gives us what is most intimate in himself, he gives us his heart. And it is only because his heart is in us that we can understand something of his love, of what he is. 'Love is from God; everyone who loves is born of God and knows

God. Whoever does not love does not know God, for God is love' (1 John 4:7–8).

Christ is the human face of God's love. 'Whoever has seen me has seen the Father' (John 14:9). The Spirit is his heart. He enters into us, he creates in us a love like his own, and having become 'perfect' like the Father, we love with his love.

> No one has ever seen God; if we love one another, God lives in us, and his love is perfected in us. By this we know that we abide in him and he in us, because he has given us of his Spirit. (1 John 4:12–13)

The Spirit does not bring us a new revelation. Everything has been given in Christ. The Spirit 'will take what is mine and declare it to you' (John 16:14). But the mystery of Christ is a mystery of love, and only love is capable, by transforming us progressively into itself, of giving us entry into it. That is the meaning of the age of the Church, of the age of worship in Spirit and in truth (John 4:23); it is the meaning of our vocation and of prayer.

> I pray that the God of our Lord Jesus Christ, the Father of glory, may give you a spirit of wisdom and revelation as you come to know him, so that, with the eyes of *your heart* enlightened, you may know . . . (Ephesians 1:17–18)

Only the heart inhabited by Love, become Love, can know God.

Those who love one another aspire to be one. By their love, they live in each other. Love transports the lover into his beloved's heart.

That affective ecstasy by its nature tends to become a real unity. Lovers seek actually to transmit their respective lives to each other and to fuse them in one single life. The kiss is a definite expression of that aspiration. The fusion of breaths signifies the fusion of lives and hearts, but cannot be realised, for in human beings the breath, although the vehicle of life, is not life itself.

In God, the kiss of love between the Father and the Son is not the expression of an aspiration, but the fruit of a perfect union. The Father and the Son are one in their single nature. The impetus of love of one towards the other is so total that it achieves the gift of their whole heart, of their whole being, of one to the other. This ecstatic gift, bearer of the divine nature, 'materialises' as the bond and pledge of the love of the Father and the Son: it is the Holy Spirit, 'the flame that shoots forth from a furnace of infinite love' (Scheeben).

Just as inevitably, his presence in our hearts creates love. Inversely, all the love there is in the universe, every desire for unity, every act of charity and tenderness, even if obscured and only partly true, every aspiration towards communion which is secretly at work, even in inanimate creation, all that is dependent on the heartbeat of him who is love. The heart of being – its ultimate secret – is love. One day all will be love.

The Holy Spirit is like an immense wave of energy which traverses the entire universe, an ebb and flow: creative love born of the Father through the Son, sanctifying love, returning to the Father through Christ, bringing everything to its consummation.

The interior Master

The Spirit dwells in our hearts. He does not remain inactive. 'For all who are *led* by the Spirit of God are children of God' (Romans 8:14). 'If we live by the Spirit, let us also be guided by the Spirit' (Galatians 5:25). We are spiritual men, in the Christian sense of the word, not to the extent that we free ourselves from the human condition, or that we become disembodied spirits through an ascetic and human effort; but to the extent that we are led by the Spirit of Christ. The spiritual life is nothing other than the life of the Holy Spirit in us.

The Spirit has two ways of leading us. He acts under the form of inspirations which manifest themselves in a twofold way. Sometimes, he simply lets us act by ourselves, make acts of the theological virtues of faith, hope and charity, or moral acts of prudence, justice, fortitude or temperance. We ourselves set these acts in motion. The Holy Spirit is not absent, he is the first cause that puts our supernatural energies into action, but we hold on to the direction, the management of our life.

That is the foundation of the Christian life: the supernatural but personal government of ourselves through the Christian virtues.

Only we possess those virtues in such an imperfect way! The exercise of the virtues suffers from the weakness of our will and our reason, even when enlightened by faith. Only the Holy Spirit is at the level of the divine life in us. That life can only blossom fully if the Spirit takes direction of it himself. This second way of leading us exists and it is guaranteed to us through what we call the seven gifts of the Holy Spirit which are infused into our souls with sanctifying grace at Baptism: gifts of the intellectual order, of wisdom, understanding, knowledge, counsel; and gifts of the order of the will, those of piety, fortitude and fear of the Lord. These gifts are interior receptivities which permit us to receive and to respond to the inspirations by which the Spirit urges and prompts us. Then we no longer have the principal role in the direction of our conduct; filled with his assistance, we have only to consent to his working.

These two ways of being led could be compared to the progress of a boat with oars or with a sail. With oars, one must work with the strength of the arms and direct the boat: one keeps the initiative. But with a sail, if the wind blows, the course no longer depends only on us; we go faster and and are not as tired.

The ordinary mode of our life is to work actively by means of the virtues, for the Spirit does not always blow (although he blows more often than not, but we do not pay attention, because we are not on the same wavelength). The Spirit's voice is gentle and discreet, and the voice of our nature speaks more loudly. And besides, we like to direct our own affairs according to our own understanding.

In short, with the years, there is a more and more marked tendency in us to listen rather to ourselves, whereas the Spirit, the Power of God, is in us. Let us resolve not to extinguish the Spirit. Let us listen to him by interior silence, humble prayer that he will guide and enlighten us, mistrust of our human strength, humility and receptivity to his delicate touches.

Indeed, one can be mistaken. We need a discernment of spirits and an apprenticeship, under the control of a human guide. But if we are faithful, our perceptive capacity will be sharpened, just as the ear of a trained musician becomes capable of picking up more and more subtle nuances of sound. When all is said and done, that is the only way to reproduce the beauty of Christ's face in us, to allow him to love and to live in us. By ourselves, we are too coarse. His Spirit, his love must live in us. The whole art of the spiritual life lies there.

The Spirit of the Son
The Spirit not only gives us additional strength, an interior direction. His action goes so far as to change our very being. He effects a second birth in us.

> 'Very truly, I tell you, no one can enter the kingdom of God without being born of water and Spirit. What is born of the flesh is flesh, and what is born of the Spirit is spirit.' (John 3:5–6)

Just as the Word of God was made flesh in Mary's womb by the action of the Holy Spirit, so the Spirit must bring about the birth of Christ in our hearts – or our birth in Christ – which amounts to the same thing.

It is a question of being born into the divine life. That can only be done by receiving a new principle of life at the same level – so it too must be divine – within us: a seed of incorruptible life sown in our human hearts.

> To all who received him [the Word made flesh], who believed in his name, he gave power to become children of God, who were born, not of blood or of the will of the flesh or of the will of man, but of God. (John 1:12–13)

This life is the divine life itself in us: indestructible life, source of all that is, perfectly transparent light, pure love in total gift: Father, Son, Holy Spirit. We have only a very, very remote idea of this prodigious exchange of personal knowledge and love which constitutes life in God. 'Now we see in a mirror, dimly' (1 Corinthians 13:12), fleeting reflections which pass like lightning, at privileged moments of love or intuition. This is spiritual life, par excellence; a life which seems so fragile, so delicate, and which, nevertheless, is stronger than death; so 'unreal', and yet it is more real than the real. And we are already living this life. Eternal life will only be the blossoming of that germ in us.

> 'Those who drink of the water that I will give them [says the Lord], will never be thirsty. The water that I will give will become in them a spring of water gushing up to eternal life.' (John 4:14)

But the image drawn from organic life shows itself to be inadequate, for that life is a life of knowledge and love between persons; between the Father and the Son and the Holy Spirit. We can only enter into it by entering into the circuit of the relationships which constitute these Persons. The Incarnate Word is the door that opens onto that life. United to the only Son who enables us to participate in his knowledge of the Father, we enter into his filial relationship with the Father; we become, in all truth, sons of God. The Spirit, bond of love between the Father and the Son, realises that union with the Son in us and draws us into the breath of love towards the Father which is his very being.

> God sent his Son, born of a woman, born under the law . . . so that we might receive adoption as children. And because you are children, God has sent the Spirit of his Son into our hearts, crying, 'Abba! Father!' (Galatians 4:4b–6)

Our adoption is not a juridical fiction, but an ontological transformation. By communicating himself to us and by dwelling in us, the Holy Spirit makes us adopted sons of God.

> You are not in the flesh; you are in the Spirit, since the Spirit of God dwells in you. Anyone who does not have the Spirit of Christ does not belong to him. (Romans 8:9)

The Father's plan from all eternity is that we be 'conformed to the image of his Son' (Romans 8:29). That conformity is realised from within by the Spirit, who is the Spirit of the

Son and can communicate the dispositions of Christ to us, by creating the filial spirit in us, not an imitation of his, but a true participation in the sonship of the only Son. We become by grace what the Son is by nature. We are, in Christ, 'participants of the divine nature' (2 Peter 1:4).

The prayer of Christ in our hearts

'The Spirit itself bears witness with our spirit that we are children of God' (Romans 8:16). Of what does this witness consist? It cannot be a question of charismatic manifestations reserved for a few, but of something that belongs in a fundamental way to every Christian life. By the gift of divine life, the adopted children are subject to the action of the Spirit: they are guided, prompted, directed by the Spirit of God (Romans 8:14; Galatians 5:18). The depth of that divine action manifests itself in a special way in prayer: assimilated to Christ, we are also assimilated to his prayer, that which he recites in us through his Spirit. By making us similar to the Son, the Spirit makes us act and pray as sons. He makes us become aware, in some way, of our adoption, of our new relationship with the Father. He teaches us interiorly to know God as a Father, and he exhorts us to invoke him as our Father, after the example of Jesus himself. By granting us to participate in his own manner of addressing God, it is his own voice that resounds in our prayer. The Spirit makes the prayer of Christ come to life again in us. That prayer transcends us, goes beyond the capacity of our heart. Therefore, 'The Spirit helps us in our weakness; for we do not know how to pray as we ought, but that very Spirit intercedes with sighs too deep for words' (Romans 8:26).

Through the prayer of Christ in us, we enter into Christ's sentiments towards his Father, we experience the heart of Christ from within; the love of Christ for the Father and for others shapes our heart. For me, that is a very important aspect of the sacrifice of the Mass, in which the supreme prayer of Christ is made present here and now. One can immerse one's own prayer in it and enter into harmony with the universal love that animates Christ. Likewise, in the prayer of the Office, in the recitation of the Psalms etc., we must be aware that it is the

Spirit of Christ who prays in us. That prayer extends beyond our individual preoccupations and our sensibility to embrace all in Christ, the whole Church which is his Body. If a member of the Church is suffering, the Spirit can give expression to that person's anguish on our lips. The same goes for supplication, adoration or praise, which the prayer of the Office expresses in turn, but which do not necessarily correspond to our subjective, personal state. But each time, they correspond to the truth of the total Christ.

Let us be keenly aware that the Spirit is present at the most intimate heart of our prayer. To recollect oneself is not to close in on oneself, but to immerse oneself in the Spirit of Christ in us, to allow the prayer of his love to gush forth in our hearts. To get into the habit, let us, at the moment of entering into prayer, be it public or private, allow the prayer of Christ to flow in us. This effects an extraordinary deepening of our prayer, and also a profound communion in the prayer of all the members of Christ. The deepest bond that unites the members of a praying community is the one Spirit that prays in them. 'Through him both of us have access in one Spirit to the Father' (Ephesians 2:18).

Let us not forget the tone of confident familiarity that the word 'Abba' evokes. It should be translated as 'Daddy', and it implies a closeness that is totally new in humans' relationship with God. Only the Spirit of Christ could form that prayer in us. 'You did not receive a spirit of slavery to fall back into fear, but you have received a spirit of adoption; when we cry, "Abba! Father!" ' (Romans 8:15).

Most often, it is not respect that we lack towards God, but audacity, confidence.

The Spirit of freedom
'Where the Spirit of the Lord is, there is freedom' (2 Corinthians 3:17). What distinguishes the son from the slave is that he is free. Freedom is one of the greatest goods that humans can possess. There is today a universal aspiration towards freedom from political, social, economic, psychological and other constraints. We are witnessing an ever deeper sensitisation

with regard to the bonds that fetter our human freedom and a relentless effort to break them. The Christian, as a human being, plays a part in this effort. But the freedom given by the Spirit of Christ is situated at a different level; it is independent of external conditioning. St Paul's surprising indifference to a person's political condition is thus accounted for: to be a slave or a free person, where civil liberty was the very basis of human dignity, that seemed immaterial to him (1 Corinthians 7:21). Christian emancipation is radical in a different way. Nor is it to be confused with the ideal of wise men, Stoics or others, who, through reflection and moral effort, sought to acquire perfect self-control and to establish themselves in an inviolable inner tranquillity.

The Christian's freedom is emancipation with regard to sin, to the law and to death. It is personal and interior, a fruit of the Spirit of Christ in us. A person can be free in a prison. Politically and socially without constraint, he can be the slave of his passions which stifle his options and force him into evil. Our selfishness, our pride, our sensibilities, our need to impose ourselves, to look well, our narrow attitudes, those are our real chains. In passing, let us note that one of the functions of monastic obedience is to free us from the tyranny of our selfishness and our whim. What we do according to our will is free. Our will is directed towards what is good. If, because of a passion or a bad disposition, we turn away from what is good, we act slavishly, because we are driven by a force external to our will. However, we are easily mistaken. We mistake what is not the true good for the good. Blind, we willingly follow the inclination of our passions. We seem to be free, but, in fact, we are the slaves of our evil passions. We are slaves too when we abstain from evil only because of a contrary, coercive law. Freedom is essentially positive. It is emancipation from fetters, but more profoundly, it is the capacity to accomplish good.

We are free when we act voluntarily through love of the *true* good. On the one hand, there is a demand for the truth. We must act with a view to the *true* good. We do not discover the knowledge of this good by a philosophical analysis. Christ reveals it to us, he who is the Truth. 'If you continue in my word, you are truly my disciples; and you will know the truth, and the truth will make you free' (John 8:31–32). The freedom of the Spirit is lucid and true. It is the power to accomplish good, the true good that the Spirit of Christ brings to our knowledge. The Christian's freedom is not independence from every law. As St Paul, that great champion of freedom, says, 'I am not free from God's law but *am under Christ's law*' (1 Corinthians 9:21).

On the other hand, there is in freedom a demand for spontaneity. We are only free when acting of our own volition. A law imposed from outside is a servitude. The freedom of the Christian consists precisely in this, that the Holy Spirit predisposes our will to do the true good, by the gentle attraction of love for that good. It is by pouring his love into our hearts that he makes us free, to follow the law of love. Whatever we do because we want to do it, we do freely, even if that is prescribed by God. Freedom is necessarily internal. 'For freedom Christ has set us free. Stand firm, therefore, and do not submit again to a yoke of slavery' (Galatians 5:1).

The Christian's relationship to the law is radically changed. We live under the regime of grace. The observance of an external law, of any external law, even given by God, as was the case for the Jews, cannot bring salvation to sinful people. Salvation is a pure grace of God, and the free accomplishment of his law is also a grace, the fruit of the action of the Spirit in us – so that no one may boast before God. Everything is grace. True freedom is humble – but it is immense! We most often get dizzy before the freedom that Christ gives us, we have not the courage to bear it, we need external supports.

'If you are led by the Spirit, you are not subject to the law' (Galatians 5:18). *If* you are led by the Spirit. That does not happen automatically. We do not receive our freedom as a boon acquired once for all. And we do not become free passively. The gift of the Spirit is rather a power to become free. It remains a task to be accomplished, by allowing the law of love to penetrate progressively and actively into every layer of our being and our activity – and that is the work of a whole lifetime.

Our freedom demands our co-operation with grace, our per-severing and laborious efforts, which express in a concrete way our constant docility to the Spirit.

> Those who belong to Christ Jesus have crucified the flesh with its passions and desires. If we live by the Spirit, let us also be guided by the Spirit. (Galatians 5:24–25)

If we look into ourselves, we can easily see the multitude of bonds that fetter the freedom of the Spirit, that hinder the blossoming of love in us. We easily confuse freedom with self-assertion, the affirmation of our egoism. But true freedom is a service of charity, of self-forgetfulness.

> For you were called to freedom, brothers and sisters; only do not use your freedom as an opportunity for self-indulgence, but through love become slaves to one another. (Galatians 5:13)

The Spirit of love who acts in us does not lead us to an isolated perfection. His action is always directed towards the growth of the whole Body of Christ, the gifts he bestows are for the good of all. We are never so free as in the renunciation of our individual freedom in order to put it at the service of our brothers.

> For though I am free with respect to all, I have made myself a slave to all ... To the weak I became weak, so that I might win the weak. I have become all things to all people, that I might by all means save some. (1 Corinthians 9:19, 22)

Where the Christian's freedom is most clearly distinguishable from every other freedom is in the emancipation from the ultimate slavery of death. In Christ we are freed from the fear of death (Hebrews 2:14) and that silent anguish that it engenders in the inmost depths of human consciousness, an anguish which more often than not does not have a name, but which is present like a sombre back-drop to the whole of life.

If the Spirit of him who raised Jesus from the dead dwells in you, he who raised Christ from the dead will give life to your mortal bodies also through his Spirit that dwells in you. (Romans 8:11)

30

Return to the Father

THE REVELATION OF THE FATHER

The image and the emotional resonances which the word 'Father' evokes for each one of us are very much conditioned by our experience vis-à-vis our earthly father. As all human beings are imperfect, we must purify our conception of what a father is in transferring it to our heavenly Father, because, at an optimistic estimate, our earthly father can only be a distant image of him who is the source of all life and all fatherhood (Ephesians 3:15). It is a more difficult but still more necessary task to free ourselves, if necessary, from the imperfect emotional attitudes of either infantile dependence or juvenile rebellion, in which our emotional development would have come to a halt before arriving at the attitude of freedom, of filial love and the responsible obedience of a person who has found his independence. That implies a moment of rupture which allows each one to find his own identity, but which must be completed by a gesture of reconciliation by which an adult relationship of love and mutual trust is established with his father. This whole process only prepares the ground on which our relationship with God the Father is built, but it is of prime importance, and there are very few people who do not suffer from a certain ambivalence, more or less repressed, with regard to the Father. That is so true that one can say to the beginner, show me your father and I will show you some characteristics of your God. Fortunately, the Spirit of the Son is there to purify what needs purification and to introduce us, little by little, to a true filial attitude. So let us look, as always, at Christ.

The Old Testament and Judaism have made known some characteristics of God the Father in his relations with humankind: his relationship of choice with the people of God as a whole, then a relationship of predilection towards the king and the just individual. But they were only faint glimmers, to prepare the way for the definitive revelation of the true divine fatherhood which appears in all its fullness in the revelation brought by the Son, living in the Father.

> 'No one knows the Son except the Father, and no one knows the Father except the Son and anyone to whom the Son chooses to reveal him.' (Matthew 11:27)

No one can arrive by his own resources at the knowledge of the Father, for knowledge is, in the last analysis, a question of being: the capacity to know is measured by what one is. Jesus reveals the Father to us, not only objectively in his person and his life, but more profoundly by making us participate in his being as Only Son through the gift of his Spirit. That, as we have seen, is the profound meaning of the prayer of Jesus in our hearts: 'Abba! Father!'

> And the Word became flesh and lived among us, and we have seen his glory, the glory as of a father's only son . . . No one has ever seen God. It is God the only Son, who is close to the Father's heart, who has made him known. (John 1:14, 18)

All Jesus' behaviour during his public ministry, his way of living, his teaching, his merciful reception of sinners, above all his love and the gift of his life for us, all of that revealed the Father. Everything spoke of the Father's incredible love for us, of his goodness, his providence, his mercy. That is only the translation onto the human level of his eternal being as Word of God, perfect expression and substantial image of the Father; Word in which the Father says all that he is. In return, the Word is turned entirely towards God, and from their communion of love the Holy Spirit flows. The supreme secret of Jesus' work is that God is his Father in the literal sense. It is by revealing him that he introduces us into the mystery of his personality and of his personal relationship with God, and at the same time he introduces us into the Mystery of the Father.

One can sense the reproach in Jesus' voice before his disciples' slowness to understand that.

'Have I been with you all this time, Philip, and you still do not know me? Whoever has seen me has seen the Father. How can you say, "Show us the Father"? Do you not believe that I am in the Father and the Father is in me?' (John 14:9–10)

'The Father and I are one.' (John 10:30)

To fail to recognise that relationship to the Father, that relationship that he *is*, eternally, is entirely to fail to recognise the Son and the Father (John 8:19).

The Father loves you

At the moment of his final farewell, Jesus makes a supreme effort. 'I will tell you plainly of the Father,' he says (John 16:25). So what is the Father's secret? It is so simple and so sublime! It is that he is a Father, that he is our Father, and that he loves us. That is how he is – the One who is, the source and end of all being and of everything. Being is kindness, the Father is Love, for in him acting and being are not distinct.

But how does one put across the sublime simplicity of that light without shadow? It is in prayer that the relationship between God and ourselves is most directly expressed. 'On that day you will ask in my name. I do not say to you that I will ask the Father on your behalf; for the Father himself loves you' (John 16:26–27).

Confidence in prayer

It is striking to see how much Jesus insists, not only in the Last Discourse in St John, but also in the Synoptics, on the confidence which ought to accompany our requests. If we were fully aware that our prayer is addressed to the Father who loves us, how could we doubt? Has he not promised, in the most explicit way possible, through the mouth of Christ?

'So I say to you, Ask, and it will be given you; search, and you will find; knock, and the door will be opened for you.

For everyone who asks receives, and everyone who searches finds, and for everyone who knocks, the door will be opened. Is there anyone among you who, if your child asks for a fish, will give a snake instead of a fish? Or if the child asks for an egg, will give a scorpion? If you then, who are evil, know how to give good gifts to your children, how much more will the heavenly Father give the Holy Spirit to those who ask him!' (Luke 11:9–13)

If at times he does not give us what we ask, our confidence in his love should be strong enough to believe that, according to God's way of seeing things, it is better for us not to receive that gift. All that we ask in Christ's name, not just by pronouncing that name materially, but in union with the Lord, the Father will give to us, as far as that ultimate gift, the Holy Spirit: that is to say, God himself communicating himself to us in love.

However, we must admit, more often than not we do not receive because we lack faith. 'If you had faith the size of a mustard seed, you could say to this mulberry tree, "Be uprooted and planted in the sea", and it would obey you' (Luke 17:6). 'Lord, increase our faith.' We are more willing to believe in the infallibility of the laws of nature, in human autonomy, in our personal unworthiness, in anything, rather than in that banking on God that ought to come from faith. The saints did otherwise.

'Lord, help my unbelief!'

The mediation of Christ
The Father loves us because we love Christ and believe in him (cf. John 16:27). Our confidence in the Father is based on our union with Christ. We pray in his name. Jesus Christ is the one Mediator between God and humankind. But Christ's mediation greatly exceeds that of a mere intermediary, like that of someone placed between God and us, or finding himself 'beside' us. He is an ontological mediator, because he is at one and the same time God and human. In him the absolute manifestation and gift of God appear. In him too, that gift is

received with perfect love. In him, finally, humanity and the entire universe are conceived, created, redeemed and sanctified. When the Father looks at us, he sees us in the Son, and he loves us. That is not an invention, an 'as if', it is the reality. In order to understand it better, we must meditate on our union with Christ. This week in which we celebrate the Ascension, the Liturgy invites us to do that; it envisages that mystery as our entry into the divine life, which is only to be understood in the mystery of our union with Christ.

UNION WITH CHRIST ACCORDING TO ST JOHN

The True Vine

The parable of the vine (John 15:1–10) occupies the centre of Jesus' farewell discourse. That is not by chance, for the union with Christ that it signifies is the centre from which springs our union with the divine Persons, our union with our brothers and our union with the universe. Everything rests on the depth of that union with Christ: either we are united to Christ as to any master, as admirable and perfect as you like, but, at the end of the day, outside us, different from us; or it is a question of an infinitely more intimate union, to the extent that the distinction between Christ and us seems to disappear, leaving only one single being. We will take as our guides St John and St Paul, or rather the Word of God who bares his heart to us in their message. The images they use are very simple. But what they try to convey is so extraordinary that we look at it without truly penetrating it. We are blinded by too much light. I ask you this time to stop, to try in a spirit of prayer and openness to grasp something of the reality of our union with Christ, which is the reality of our spiritual life.

'I am the true vine, you are the branches' (John 15:1, 5). Everything is already there, I am not the stem of the vine and you the branches. No, I am the whole vine; and nevertheless, you are the branches. So, you are a part of what I am; together we form a single living organism.

Here Jesus goes beyond his human individuality in order to reveal himself as a collective and yet perfectly one 'living reality' who includes within himself the whole of regenerated humanity. It is as if the divine person of the Word were prolonging his incarnation from the stem, which is the man Jesus, all the way into the branches, the living unity of the whole forming the total Christ. It is through Jesus alone that the vine draws from the heart of the divine life, and the life of God pours out into all the branches so that they may live by it.

Abide in me

'Those who abide in me and I in them bear much fruit, because apart from me you can do nothing' (John 15:5). Christ is the place of our abode, of our repose. To abide. The word evokes a solid, lasting adherence in faith to Christ, and a certain intimate presence born of love and mutual knowledge. 'Abide in me as I abide in you' (15:4). So, that depends on us. We must set about it actively and constantly. Our union with Christ must be sustained consciously by a habit of recollection. We must immerse ourselves as often as possible in Christ in whom we live, under the influence of his Spirit in us. All that we do, we should do in Christ; let us stop for a moment before beginning an activity, so that it may always flow from our union with him. Let us love our brothers in Christ, for they also are Christ (Matthew 25:31–46), and we love them with his love. May all our judgements be those of Christ, let us look at everything through his eyes. May it be his prayer that wells up from our heart, his praise that sings in our voices. May it be his Cross that we carry, and his life and his joy that are in us. 'As the Father has loved me, so I have loved you; abide in my love' (15:9).

Our effort will not be in vain, for it is founded on his presence in us, on his Spirit in us, on the fidelity of his love. Jesus *abides* in us, peacefully, profoundly, source of life, of action and love. The sap of his life that flows in us is a sap of love and light; the fruit that it will produce in abundance are the works of a true and efficacious love, and a unity of love between us, the branches, in him.

'Apart from me you can do nothing' (15:5). Nothing, absolutely nothing. Let us be firmly convinced of that truth. Apart from Christ, the most strenuous efforts cannot have any success. In him, everything is possible: love, unity, eternal life.

To bear fruit

The mystical presence is only true if it produces fruit in abundance. If our efforts to abide in Christ only result in rendering us self-centred, irritable, suspicious and critical towards our brothers, it is greatly to be feared that it is not in Christ that we abide, but in the citadel of our isolated ego whose motto is 'All for me, and me above all'.

Truly to 'abide in Christ' is 'to abide in his love' (15:9). And, 'If you keep my commandments, you will abide in my love . . . This is my commandment, that you love one another as I have loved you' (15:10a, 12).

If it is not possible to love without doing good, it is possible to do good without loving. There is a heresy of 'do-gooders' (those who reduce religion to the service of others). The external service of another can be a way of escaping the demands of an interior love, or an effort to fill a personal emptiness by the appropriation of another, an enslavement of the object of a 'charity' in which there is a strong element of self-affirmation.

Love is, in the first place, something that belongs to the heart. It is the welcoming of another precisely as other, the joyful acceptance of the fact that he is and that he is as he is. It is to delight in him, it is to be able to see through his eyes, to put him at the centre of a vision of the world in the same way as we spontaneously put ourselves at the centre of our world. It is to desire his welfare efficaciously, in deed and in truth. It is to give oneself, like Christ.

UNION WITH CHRIST ACCORDING TO ST PAUL

As many of you as were baptized into Christ have clothed yourselves with Christ. There is no longer Jew or Greek, there is no longer slave or free, there is no longer male and female; for all of you are one in Christ Jesus. (Galatians 3:27–28)

Our incorporation into Christ occurs at Baptism, the sacrament of faith. Paul presents that incorporation here under the image of putting on a garment. Elsewhere he uses more striking comparisons: immersed by Baptism in Christ, we are 'buried with him', 'united with him in a death like his' in order also to be united with him in a resurrection like his (cf. Romans 6:3–11). One can say that, as at the Baptism of Jesus in the Jordan, at every Baptism the Father declares through his Spirit to every baptised person: 'You are my Son, the Beloved; with you I am well pleased' (Mark 1:11).

All of us are but one in Jesus Christ. How does one understand this 'one'? St Thomas, the most measured of theologians, does not hesitate to understand it as 'as it were a single mystical person'.* In order to grasp the force of the expression, one has to recall the multiple ways in which St Paul tried to express the union between Christ and us. We have been 'engendered in Christ' (1 Corinthians 4:15), 'rooted and built up in him' (Colossians 2:7), 'come to fullness in him' (2:10); we are 'in Christ' (1 Corinthians 1:30; cf. 1 Peter 5:14; 1 John 5:20) and 'Christ is in us' (2 Corinthians 13:5; Romans 8:10; Colossians 1:27). Christ is the source and the permanent principle of our new life as children of God (Galatians 4:5). He is present in us as a vivifying and active power (Colossians 1:29; Philippians 4:13; 2 Corinthians 12:9 etc.) to the extent that Paul can exclaim: 'It is no longer I who live, but it is Christ who lives in me' Galatians 2:20). In a word, 'For to me, living is Christ' (Philippians 1:21).

Those phrases are not just a matter of style. They are, rather, stammerings of language, unable to express a reality that infinitely surpasses his power of expression. And that reality is ours. We must become ever more imbued with the awareness of the depth of our union with Christ. Christ is formed in us through his Spirit (Galatians 4:19). We have become new men (Ephesians 4:24), new creatures formed in the image of the only Son (Romans 8:29), it is the life of Jesus that animates our bodies (2 Corinthians 4:10).

---

* S.T. IIIa, Q.48.a.2: quasi una persona mystica.

One can see from what depths and with what truth our prayer to the Father springs forth. It is Jesus who is its principle, it is he who, praying his own prayer in us, gives us a share in it. And because of our mystical identification with Christ, that prayer is ours, the truth of our new being.

By virtue of our union with Christ, every difference between us, religious and social as well as natural, disappears. That is another truth of which we must become more aware. We are usually so superficial that we stop at all kinds of external differences, bodily and social qualities, nationality, culture etc. We keep our charity confined in sealed containers, while the love of Christ in us is so vigorous that it wants to embrace everyone and penetrate to the heart of everyone, there where everyone is the image and child of God. We form a brotherhood bound by ties that are even deeper than blood ties. In Christ and through him, we form a single body animated by the same life: Christ is the head, we are his members (1 Corinthians 12:12ff; Colossians 1:22) and, consequently, 'members of one another' (Ephesians 4:25), each one responsible for his part of the whole body. Each member finds the meaning and perfection of his being and activity only in terms of his place in the body.

> But speaking the truth in love, we must grow up in every way into him who is the head, into Christ, from whom the whole body, joined and knit together by every ligament with which it is equipped, as each part is working properly, promotes the body's growth in building itself up in love.
> (Ephesians 4:15–16)

Individually and collectively, to be ourselves is to arrive at 'the measure of the full stature of Christ' (Ephesians 4:13).

The exaltation of Christ
No one has celebrated the Paschal triumph of Christ with the same amplitude as has St Paul. It is a mystery in which the omnipotence of the Father is manifest.

> [I pray ... that you may know] what is the immeasurable greatness of his power for us who believe, according to the

working of his great power. God put this power to work in
Christ when he raised him from the dead and seated him
at his right hand in the heavenly places, far above all rule
and authority and power and dominion, and above every
name that is named, not only in this age but also in the
age to come. (Ephesians 1:19–21)

Those are the true dimensions of Christ's exaltation. And that
concerns us, for we are the members of his body, we are 'the
full stature' of Christ, as St Paul expresses it.

And he has put all things under his feet and has made him
the head over all things for the church, which is his body,
the fullness of him who fills all in all. (Ephesians 1:22–23)

We must not imagine that the Church is Christ's complement,
that is to say, something added to him. The Church is the
fullness (*pleroma*) of Christ in the sense that it is filled with
the riches of the divine life through Christ, who is himself filled
with God (Colossians 2:9–17). It seems that the whole universe,
assumed into Christ's glorification, should be included in that
fullness which is Christ's. In any case, it is clear that Christ's
glory pours onto all things and especially onto his Church. In
Christ, we have already entered into the divine life.

God, who is rich in mercy, out of the great love with
which he loved us even when we were dead through our
trespasses, made us alive together with Christ – by grace
you have been saved – and raised us up with him and
seated us with him in the heavenly places in Christ Jesus.
(Ephesians 2:4–6)

More even than an event, the solemnity of the Ascension
celebrates a mystery, that of the fulfilment of the Passover in
the entire Body of Christ, head and members. By entering into
heaven, Christ 'raised our frail human nature to glory' (Roman
Canon). 'He was raised up into heaven so that he might make
us . . . sharers in his Godhead' (Preface of the Ascension). 'Our
life is hidden with Christ in God' (Colossians 3:3). From this

moment onwards, we can only tend with all our strength towards our true homeland. We belong to that land.

> So if you have been raised with Christ, seek the things that are above, where Christ is, seated at the right hand of God. Set your minds on things that are above, not on things that are on earth. (Colossians 3:1–2)

We have already meditated on that text and I will not return to it except to say that it is not a question of evading the human condition, a sort of imaginary compensation for what is lacking in our life. The present life retains all its seriousness, and we should devote ourselves honestly to our worldly tasks. It must even be said that those tasks acquire all their seriousness only in the light of the eternal life for which they prepare us, in the sense that the way we live our life here below determines our eternal destiny. The love and the faith we exercise on earth will be the measure of our participation in the divine bliss. We will appear before God with the heart we will have made for ourselves, with the capacity for love and light that we will have hollowed out in it.

THE ASCENSION

Christ's return to the Father seems to be realised in a manner that is open to view, in the Ascension described by the Synoptics. We encounter a difficulty here: the difference between the chronological framework adopted by St John and by St Luke in the Acts.

St John does not separate the Resurrection from Christ's Exaltation, thus expressing the inner unity of the Paschal mystery. He does not give any description of a visible ascension of Christ to heaven.

St Luke describes the Ascension twice, first of all at the end of his Gospel (Luke 24:50–53), then in the first chapter of the Acts of the Apostles (Acts 1:6–11). In the first account, St Luke presents the Ascension on the night or the morrow of Easter, thus agreeing with St John in the essentials; in the second account the Ascension takes place forty days after Easter. Do we have to choose between these dates?

The early Christian theologians, the majority of the witnesses, place the Ascension of the Lord on Easter day itself. Theologically, it is the only suitable solution. Jesus does not wait in a cave in Jerusalem for the gate of heaven to be opened. From the moment he emerges from death, he enters into life. So what becomes of the Ascension from the Mount of Olives described in the Acts? It remains as the final departure. Jesus, having entered into the world of the Resurrection, still manifests himself mysteriously in our world, or better, puts himself within the reach of our senses during a period of apparitions. It was in order to prove that he was alive, to instruct his disciples and to lay a foundation for the authority of their testimony, for this period ends with the sending of the disciples on a mission into the whole world.

That period came to an end. The final farewell, the final apparition after Easter received the title of Ascension and St Luke places it forty days after Easter. It seems clear that the number forty expresses the idea of a certain plenitude, as is usual in the Bible.

For St Luke it was a question of, first of all in Luke 24, ending a Gospel account, then in Acts 1, of beginning a history of the Church. The perspective is not the same, but the realities expressed are not contradictory. What is essential is the glorification of Jesus in his humanity, often expressed in the New Testament by the image of accession to the right hand of God, borrowed from Psalm 110:1. That heavenly exaltation is inseparable from the Resurrection. It is a mystery accessible only to faith. The sensible manifestation crowning the series of post-Easter Christophanies is an event which, of itself, falls within the sphere of human testimony and its historical consistency is independent of that of Christ's exaltation. It seems evident that the images used by Luke are highly stylised: the clouds of heaven, the angels who give the theological interpretation of the event, that is to say the passage from the time of Jesus visibly present to the time of the Church and the Apostles. We must resist a double temptation: sterile regret for the past, or fanciful contemplation of the future. It is up to us to accomplish the task for which we are responsible in the present, in love and faith, not without the assurance that the Lord will manifest himself at the appointed time and that he remains present in his Church. 'I am with you always, to the end of the age' (Matthew 28:20).

The Church's great task is to bear witness to what it has seen: 'Go into all the world and proclaim the good news to the whole creation' (Mark 16:15). But for that it needs the power of the Spirit, and Christ says: 'And see, I am sending upon you what my Father promised; so stay here in the city until you have been clothed with power from on high' (Luke 24:49).

THE PRAYER OF JESUS (JOHN 17:1–26)

This prayer has a very meticulous literary structure. One can distinguish three parts in it which correspond to the three great requests that Jesus addresses to his Father. He asks him for: his own glorification (1–8); the sanctification of the disciples (9–19); the realisation of the mystery of the unity of love in the whole Church (20–26).

It is the whole economy of salvation in the form of a prayer. It is also like the Ascension of Jesus in prayer, and that is why the Liturgy reads the first two parts of it in the week preceding the feast of the Ascension, and the final part during the time between the Ascension and Pentecost.

It is very difficult to comment on this prayer: either one says too much and one breaks up into pieces what is a living movement, or one just repeats what is best said in the prayer itself. For rather than a prose passage, a logical sequence of ideas, it is a question of a poetic entity that has its own life and beauty, and that cannot be reduced to the ideas it expresses.

One can only invite each person to read this prayer with his heart, in a profound spirit of recollection. It must be read several times until the rhythm of its movement enters into our hearts and the glory of Jesus carries us into the knowledge-love of the Father, from whom every gift comes, and first of all the gift of his love and of faith in Christ. Then we must let the truth

of Christ in us guard us – we who are not of the world but who
are in this world – guard us by sanctifying us in the Truth that
he communicates to us by his sacrifice. We must let the
immense energy of Christ's love, of his joy, blossom out in us,
to embrace all people in the unity of love, a unity which is the
prolongation in this world of the essential unity between
the Father and the Son through the bond of their love. Thus
is consummated the assumption into Christ of humanity and
of the universe and their entry into the divine, eternal life, their
return to the Origin, to the Father. In Christ we will be one,
we will know and love with his knowledge and love, for all
eternity.

Love is God's final word, the fruit of the knowledge of the
Father that Christ brings to us and that the Spirit realises in
us.

> 'Father . . . I made your name known to them, and I will
> make it known, so that the love with which you have loved
> me may be in them, and I in them.' (John 17:26)

That is Jesus' prayer at the moment of his departure: 'I am
coming to you, [Father]' (17:11). But we know that 'Jesus
Christ is the same, yesterday, today and for ever'. His prayer is
eternally present before the Father in the glorified humanity of
his Son who still bears the stigmata of his Passion. That mute
supplication calls for the gift of the Spirit who will achieve the
work of the unity of love in the Church and in all humankind.
Therefore, we should never lose confidence, never doubt that
God's plan is fulfilled and will be fulfilled, even if we cannot
detect the hidden ways in which he is at work. Everything
that tends to realise the prayer of Christ is the work of his
Spirit.

As our part is to be God's collaborators principally through
prayer and a hidden love, it is the Spirit who forms the prayer
of Christ in us. We should let ourselves be moulded by it, let
our attitudes be formed according to it, let our hearts widen to
its dimension. There is nothing complicated or esoteric. All
that is needed is an immense love.

The Holy Spirit is not named in this prayer, but he is con-

stantly present, for it is he who is the source of love in our
hearts (17:26). That is why our desire that the prayer of Jesus
be fulfilled in the world becomes, on our part, a prayer for the
gift of the Spirit.

31

Jesus, High Priest

In the days of his flesh, Jesus offered up prayers and supplications, with loud cries and tears, to the one who was able to save him from death, and he was heard because of his reverent submission. Although he was a Son, he learned obedience through what he suffered; and having been made perfect, he became the source of eternal salvation for all who obey him, having been designated by God a high priest according to the order of Melchizedek.

(Hebrews 5:7–10)

Christ alone is the priest of the new covenant in the fullness of priesthood. He alone is the mediator, his sacrifice is unique, has no need to be repeated (unlike the sacrifices of the Old Testament). The redemption he brings is definitive, and brings us into the definitive life.

All that remains to be done is to re-present his eternal sacrifice, to re-actualise it in time, so that it is accessible to all throughout the ages. That happens in the sacrifice of the Mass. To this end, Christ calls and gives certain members of his Church a special participation in his authority and power, and appoints them, by an infusion of his Spirit, through the hands of his Church, as priests (ministerial) in a specific and particular capacity for the service of their brothers and the glory of the Father. To be precise: the ministerial priest represents, renders Christ present in his role as mediator, he does not take his place. There is only one Priest in the New Covenant.

THE CHRISTIAN PRIEST

The Christian, every Christian, from his Baptism, is a priest in so far as he participates in Christ's priesthood, hence in so far as he participates in the risen humanity of Christ in the Spirit, and as his being and his entire life are transformed into it. In him we ought to find the same keynotes as in Christ.

The Christian is a priest

- as a human being, in all the dimension of his humanity, in all his human density, that is to say, not only in his soul, but also in his flesh, and his heart. He stands, for good or evil, together with all his brothers and sisters.

- as child of God, begotten anew by the baptismal water and the gift of the Spirit, already risen with Christ in faith. As son, he enters into Christ's movement towards the Father, by opening himself up to him, by letting himself be transformed by the Spirit deeply rooted in his heart, from where he prays within: 'Father'. As child, he has the power to 'worship the living God' (Hebrews 9:14), offering a sacrifice of praise, a song of silent adoration, not only a ritual activity (this has its place), but his whole life transformed by the priestly love of Christ.

That love manifests itself:

- by his filial obedience to God, as far as the total gift of himself, placing his whole human existence at the Father's disposal for the glory of God and the salvation of his brothers and sisters;

- by his openness to his brothers, the solidarity of destiny with them, lived in compassion, prayer, intercession, mutual aid: consumed, offered for them, to them, in the Spirit;

- by his entry into intimacy with the Father, with the trust of a son who knows himself to be welcomed without condition, loved for what he is.

All that is the reality of every Christian, called by his Baptism to realise in his life that participation in Christ's priesthood which we call the common priesthood. The monastic life can be understood as a way of living this priesthood.

Monastic life and priesthood

The keynotes that characterise the monk are: unity, universality, eternity, just like Christ, just like the Christian. Here we are at the point of intersection of the Christian life, the monastic life and the priesthoods, common and ministerial. The monastic life can be understood as a priestly reality in its totality, in the sense of a transformation of the whole of life by the priestly love of Christ. The ministerial priesthood is at the service of that.

The monk is one, at least in name and in intention. He is a man who has chosen a single goal, the love of God and his neighbour. And he has chosen a very precise form of life, in which everything is ordered as directly as possible to that goal. He effects a strong concentration of all his strength in a single direction, to the exclusion of secondary goals. Hence a great simplicity, unity and life-energy.

Separated from all, united to all, the monk, above all the solitary, needs large horizons. His gaze, freed from the constraints of limited tasks, tends to reach ever wider circles. His heart wants to expand to the dimensions of Christ's heart, to embrace all human beings without distinction. In this, the monk concurs with the priestly prayer which is intended in the first place for all humankind. The particular intentions that the priest can mention in the celebration of the Mass are not the principal object of the intercession of the Mass. For certain Carthusians, that universal openness is very important and lived intensely. Compassion, intercession, presence, communion, praise, form his heartbeats.

The Risen Christ has entered into the Glory of God. He has brought there his humanity and all humankind. Our fleeting and inconstant efforts are founded on the rock of his eternal sacrifice, eternally offered.

Our wavering prayer is rooted in the prayer of him who is

always heard 'because of his reverent submission' (Hebrews 5:7), because of his love as Son. The Father hears us always, for the Son's voice is identical with his own.

Our obscure contemplation is nevertheless a participation in Christ's face to face communion with the Father, in the eternal love who is Spirit. The only difference is the hidden mode of our faith on earth. We really enter into the Glory of God, we know him as he is in himself, we love him with his own love.

The monk is called in an urgent way to enter into intimacy with the Father. That is the life of prayer. The man of the desert, in particular, is invited to pass through the true tent and to penetrate into the Holy of Holies; no idol is permitted there, and the Glory of God sits enthroned in all its mystery and majesty.

We are called to enter into the true sanctuary, beyond every image, every representation, through the true tent of encounter with God. This tent is the glorified body of Christ.

> But when Christ came as a high priest of the good things that have come, then through the greater and perfect tent (not made with hands, that is, not of this creation), he entered once for all into the Holy Place, not with the blood of goats and calves, but with his own blood, thus obtaining eternal redemption. (Hebrews 9:11–12)

The Christian priest, in Christ, enters into the divine Glory as it truly is in itself, through the eternally immolated body of the glorified Christ sacramentally rendered present. The monk, man of the desert and of prayer, man of the prayer of the desert, often man of the desert of prayer, also seeks to enter into the true Glory of the Father, beyond every image, every figure, with a proximity as total as possible between offering and acceptance. And the living way that he follows is the same. It is that of the mystery of Christ, of his death, resurrection and ascension really lived in his humanity: real death, truly risen life, transforming a man's body and heart in the fire of the Spirit.

In order to penetrate into the true sanctuary, we must die to 'our' prayer, pass through a tent not made with hands, that does not belong to this creation. We must receive from God the passage that is realised in the humanity of the glorified Christ and is communicated to us in the sacrament of faith. We need to receive the prayer of Christ by being transformed by his death into his risen state, realised in our life and in our whole being. Thus we will have access, in the Spirit, to the Father's face, to intimacy with him, to his Glory, radically other, radically close.

The plunge of adoration into the silence of the mystery of God is one of the ways, it seems to me, in which the life of the monk, and especially the solitary, highlights certain aspects of priesthood.

Another aspect would be a totally open love in a radical poverty, arms stretched out over the whole of humankind, totally given in a very simple surrender.

Also, perhaps, the transparency of life, of joy in life, of something of the light of the risen humanity of Christ-Priest.

This could be the Christian root of a certain cosmic priesthood which gives voice to the praise and adoration of the universe in all its created splendour. The solitary, above all, cannot leave the earth and the heavens without a voice for God.

Finally, the expectation of the full realisation of salvation, nourished by the sacramental memorial, is lived intensely in the heart of a prayer straining unreservedly towards the invisible light, quenched by an obscure water that only makes his thirst for love all the more acute.

Maranatha! Come, Lord Jesus!

32

Waiting for the Spirit (1)

Eastertide is the celebration of Christ's victory, of the fullness of salvation. At first glance, it could seem strange that the final part of this time is given over to waiting for the Spirit. But it is nothing of the sort.

On the pragmatic level, the suppression of the Octave of Pentecost which was detrimental to the integrity of the fifty days of Easter, entailed the suppression of a certain number of rich texts and musical pieces on the Holy Spirit. The Congregation of Rites suggested that we use them instead in the time between the Ascension and Pentecost, when they could express and revive our expectation of the gift of the Spirit at Pentecost.

At a deeper level, this time reflects the eschatological dimension of the Paschal mystery and, consequently, the incomplete character of the realisation of salvation in our world and in us. The full triumph is reserved for the last days, for the Parousia of Christ when the Church will have reached its full complement, and time will pass into eternity. Until then, the Church will always remain in pilgrimage. Therefore, she possesses Christ's riches in faith and in a hope that is straining towards an end beyond her reach. She only receives her daily bread and must walk through time in a dependence on God that never ceases.

PILGRIMS

It is the same for each one of us. United to Christ, seated in heaven with him, animated by his Spirit, sons in the Son, we are so in faith and hope, and we must walk through time, in all the fragility of our freedom, towards the homeland to which we already belong in the depths of our heart. The energy that carries us towards the Father is the energy of the Spirit. The realisation of what we are in Christ, and the meaning of our pilgrimage in this world find expression spontaneously in an ardent expectation of the Holy Spirit: may he come to fill us more and more with divine energy and love! We received the Spirit in the sacrament of Baptism, but we can always receive him more profoundly.

> Come, Holy Spirit, into our hearts,
> and send from heaven height
> a beam of your radiant Light.

The world in which we live is torn by hate and fratricidal war. Instead of a community of love, one too often finds the aggressive confrontation of blind egoisms. There is such darkness in people's minds, and so little love, that it is obvious that the Kingdom of God is not fully established on earth. Rather, it is like a tiny grain that is in danger of being trampled under oblivious feet. This seed is also suffocated in our hearts; yes, even in us monks, whose life, however, only has meaning as a realisation, as perfect as possible, of Christ's Kingdom, and whose heart should be God's seat, a living centre of peace, prayer and the love of God and others. So, let us cry out our need and our thirst. Come, Spirit, give life to the dried-up bones that we are (Ezekiel 37:1–14), permeate our hearts with the fire of your love. We do not possess the money of merit, we have wasted God's gifts. However, let us put our trust in God's promise and ask for our bread to eat (Isaiah 55:1–2), and for that living water that flows from the throne of God and of the Lamb (Revelation 22:1–5), to quench our thirst.

BIRTH FROM THE SPIRIT

> O Blessed Light,
> come and fill
> the innermost hearts of your faithful.

'No one can enter the kingdom of God without being born of water and Spirit' (John 3:5). That birth lasts during our whole lifetime on earth, and even in heaven it will only be complete when the total Christ is realised at the end of time. The Spirit forms Christ in us, little by little, as he fashioned the humanity of Jesus in Mary's womb. The trials of this life are the pangs of our birth to true life, to love. The Father brings forth Christ in our hearts, a mysterious participation in the eternal generation of the Son.

> For this reason I bow my knees before the Father, from whom every family in heaven and on earth takes its name. I pray that, according to the riches of his glory, he may grant that you may be strengthened in your inner being with power through his Spirit, and that Christ may dwell in your hearts through faith, as you are being rooted and grounded in love. (Ephesians 3:14–17)

CHRIST'S PROMISES

We read again on the seventh Sunday (John 14:15–21) and as a ferial reading (John 14:23–29), Christ's promises. From the Father's presence, he will send 'another Advocate' (14:16) who will remain with us, to strengthen and enlighten us. And Christ will come to us, and also the Father, in a marvellous compenetration of love (14:23). 'You will know [not by hearsay, but by experience] that I am in my Father, and you in me, and I in you' (14:20); I who love you as the Father loves you; and I will reveal myself to you (14:21).

Why does this intimacy of love and knowledge with the divine persons, so clearly promised, seem to be realised so little in many of us? Of course, God is master of his gifts and he gives his mystical graces to whom he wishes. However, we do not get the impression here of something extraordinary. That should be the normal fruit of a vital adherence in faith to Christ, which should prove true for every Christian according to the extent of his love. Certainly, there is a rhythm of light and darkness – that is the normal law of our psychology; there are more or less lengthy periods of trials according to God's plan for each one; but that intimacy should be realised somewhere in our life and not only in a region of 'pure faith'. No more than in the domain of pure sensibility, of course. Let us say rather that we should sometimes have a certain experience of God through the supernaturalised 'senses', through faith, and of that divine indwelling, in so far as it exists in us.

> Come to us, Father of the poor,
> come, Light of our hearts.

Are our faith and love so poor? Do we belong so little to that world that we are unable to perceive it? Note that the divine indwelling is linked to the love we have for Christ and to the observance of the commandment of love towards our neighbour and towards God (14:15 and 21). 'If you love me' (14:15). Only he who loves in deed and in truth can experience the presence of the Father and the Son. For only he possesses that connaturality with God that allows one to know him; for we can only know that which we resemble in some way. It is the Holy Spirit, the bond of love between the Father and the Son, who infuses his love into our hearts and makes us like God and capable of knowing and loving him.

From the depth of our estrangement and poverty, we can only echo the inspiration that traverses the whole of creation, a creation which, in the final analysis, is a part of us as we form part of it.

> The whole creation has been groaning in labour pains until now; and not only the creation, but we ourselves, who have the first fruits of the Spirit, groan inwardly while we wait for adoption, the redemption of our bodies. For in hope we were saved . . . if we hope for what we do not see, we wait for it with patience. (Romans 8:22–25)

To be a human being before God, is to be straining towards the Elusive. It is to drink and to be eternally thirsty. At times it is to feel the Presence only in the emptiness of absence. It is to love in the suffering of not being love. It is to hope against all hope. It is never knowing if one possesses all or nothing. It is to be a mute cry. Towards God? Simply a mute cry.

Our Father, who art in heaven,
Hallowed be thy name;
Thy Kingdom come;
Thy will be done on earth as it is in heaven.

ECCLESIAL EXPECTATION

The expectation of the Spirit should not just be for ourselves personally, but for all humankind. Our prayer, if it is truly the prayer of the Spirit in us, will be a prayer that the Spirit may fill the world and humankind with his peace, his joy, his freedom, his love. We should bear in our hearts the anguish of sin, of non-love, and hence the absence of the Holy Spirit in the hearts of so many people. Do we know what it is to pray for our brothers? Is it simply to formulate requests to God, even with fervour, but from a distance, as if seated in an armchair, well sheltered: we the 'saved', they the 'sinners'? Is it not rather to assume their estrangement, their very real poverty, their sin? Are we in fact something different? Is it not to tearfully pray the prayer of the true beggar who is in all reality lower than all, to suffer at being so far from God, so bereft of goodness and love, to cry out to the Spirit who can save us and transform us into Christ, ourselves, our brothers and all creation? One does not pray from the comfort of an armchair. One prays with the arms of one's heart open wide on the Cross. 'To pray for mankind means: to give one's own heart's blood' (Silouan).

Sometimes in books the contemplative life is put forward as an ever more luminous penetration into God. That is true, but to the extent that the life of prayer entails an ever deeper assumption of sinful humanity into our prayer, it could be that it also demands a spiritual poverty lived ever more really, those tears that should flow down our cheeks at the thought of the world's misery. Is it possible that the failure of our 'ambitions' for sanctity might be our most authentic prayer? Again, we must live that in the confidence of faith and the surrender of love. That would be the prayer of Lazarus.

A QUESTION THAT ARISES

However, I am not too satisfied with that way of viewing the matter. That might only be a more or less unconscious rationalisation on the part of my mediocrity.

Everywhere in the world today the Spirit is blowing. One can indeed have reservations with regard to such or such individual case, but it seems impossible to deny the global fact. Something is stirring in the old Church. Something of the intoxicating enthusiasm of the beginning is animating some of its members. One speaks of a Renewal in the Spirit. Young people feel themselves swept along by the Spirit, they praise God without inhibition, manifest a great thirst for the Word of God, seem to be transformed, at time work miracles, speak different languages. Everywhere, small groups are forming, somewhat on the edge of the Church's institutions, but not in opposition to it. It is rather a question of a ferment of life in the Church's bosom.

The old campaigners of the spiritual life, the professionals of sanctity and prayer, those who have worked the whole day, are a bit scandalised: the gifts of the Holy Spirit are not the affair of first-comers, of amateurs. One needs to have toiled for a long time, to have passed through the purgative way, to be subject to a strict, ascetic discipline, to be, for greater certainty, a religious – at least, to be strictly guided, controlled by priests, people who have studied, who are experts in the delicate secrets of the life of prayer, that is so full of all kinds of snares that one does not depart from the most ordinary and most ordered way without running great risks. Above all do not trust emotions! True devotion is the laborious uprightness of the will, itself under the supervision of a very elaborate theological system. One must be able to hold out, to fulfil one's duty of prayer in dryness, even in moments of distaste.

Among the professionals, most often one does not see emotional outpourings, but rather, the arid accomplishment of a duty to pray. They know the risk of a rigid formalism in long, fixed prayers, in the execution of minutely detailed rubrics repeated every day. In spite of their efforts, they must admit, they often succumb to it. However, according to them, it is not so serious: it is the intention of the will that counts. Their slightly mechanical, quite dry, often drowsy prayer, is a public prayer, an official act of the Church, even if they do not succeed in breathing a personal life into it. Are they right?

THE INSTITUTION

All that is just like the whole of religious life. There is no room for a lot of imagination or sentimentality in the monastic life. Everything is regulated, everything is foreseen. Our fathers have carried out the same little series of exercises since the eleventh century. How would you want everything not to be regulated and foreseen? We have only to drink from the fountain of a many-centuries-old tradition, to let ourselves be formed in the mould handed down to us.

One easily conceives this monastic life on the model of a civil society, or even of the army. Energy of the will, discipline, order, obedience – those are the necessary virtues. A soldier does his duty, he does not complain. He will have his reward, for the Lord is just.

All of these things are true values, but, fundamentally, are they religious values? The deep moments of faith, the face to face encounter with him who loves us, the absolute poverty which possesses neither virtue nor merit, the tears of compassion, the praise born of wonder, before the goodness and greatness of God, the passion of a heart that loves Christ, the keen affections for our neighbour which Christ commands and which the Spirit gives: all that is not excluded, but it is not regarded as the essential. It is additional. It is even more meritorious, they say, more secure, to walk the arid ways of pure faith and blameless voluntarism. (Needless to say, this is something of a caricature.)

THE LETTER AND THE SPIRIT

The Church describes the monastic life as a sign of the Kingdom of God, kingdom of salvation, of peace, of communion, of joy. A sign that is not seen externally is no longer a sign. The first Christians stood out because of their brotherly love, their virtue, their patience in persecution, their charity towards their persecutors.

We are reproached, we are the first to reproach ourselves, that our charity does not radiate enough. We are too closed in upon ourselves, too selfish perhaps. The breath of life does not seem to succeed at all in animating the rusty wheels of the weighty mechanism of our observances, which are perhaps too venerable and too minutely detailed.

Young people only see the rigid exterior of the institutional machine. They do not feel much of the warmth of the charity that should animate it. They suffocate. They feel isolated, and not loved for themselves, as persons. Their whole culture leads them to refuse to be absorbed by 'the big machine' of any institution whatsoever. They do not accept that authority should impose the 'prefabricated' mould of tradition on them. They need to discover the values of our life for themselves. For that they need the witness of surroundings which embody these values. Young people only trust what can be directly experienced. Lofty spiritual opinions, profound theological justifications, massive quotations from the Popes and from the early tradition, all that is in danger of being labelled as ideology unless they can see and feel the love of God in our liturgical prayer and in their personal prayer; the joy and peace of the Spirit on our faces; the love of neighbour in the welcome they receive from us; and in the warmth, the thoughtfulness, the solidarity, the affection that should reign in our fraternal relations, the assumption of all humankind with whom they feel in solidarity, towards whom they feel themselves responsible. In a word, if the Spirit does not *visibly* live in the letter of our observances, they will not accept those observances. If the Gospel of Christ does not take a *concrete form* among us, it is no use – no one today will be convinced.

BE CONVERTED

It seems to me that we must hear in those very simple and intransigent demands, the voice of the Spirit: 'Be converted.' After all, we are only called upon to be what we profess and what we wish to be: men totally permeated and transformed by the Spirit of Christ, and radiating his love. We are placed before the fundamental dialectic of faith: on the one hand, our powerlessness, our sin, our failure; on the other hand, the gratuitous gift of salvation, the conversion of the old man into the new man who is Christ, by the power of the Spirit of love who is given to us. Only the Spirit can transform us, all our efforts will be useless without him. So we can only turn to him with an earnest and very humble prayer.

Come, Spirit of love, pour that love we lack into our hearts. You know that we want to love, that we want to be a light for others, for the honour of our Saviour. By embracing monastic life, each one of us sought to realise the Kingdom of Christ in his heart, in his prayer and in his fraternal relations. 'Come, Holy Spirit!'

> Without your divine power,
> there is nothing in any man,
> nothing that is not corrupt.
>
> Wash what is soiled,
> flood what is arid,
> heal what is wounded.
>
> Make supple what is stiff,
> warm up what is cold,
> put right what is distorted.

EUCHARISTIC EPICLESIS

Every day at Mass we implore the coming of the Holy Spirit, twice: once over the offerings of bread and wine so that they may become the Body and Blood of Christ; once, after the Consecration, so that the communion in the Body and Blood of the Lord may truly make us 'one body, one spirit in Christ'

(Eucharistic Prayer III), 'a living sacrifice of praise' to the glory of the Father (Eucharistic Prayer IV). It is the Holy Spirit who effects the mystery of the consecration and transformation, not only of the eucharistic gifts, but also of us who share in them, us as changed into the Body of Christ. The Holy Spirit is the operating force of the mystery of God's love. Let us make our own, every day, the prayer of the Church: that the Spirit may transform the offering of our good will and of our heart (which is too poor) into the love and the heart of Christ.

Come, Holy Spirit, fill the hearts of your faithful
and enkindle in them the fire of your Love.

Let us never separate Christ from his Spirit. Where Christ is, there is his Spirit. Christ on the Cross offered himself to the Father through the Spirit. It is by the power of the Spirit that the sacrifice of the Mass is offered by the Church. It is the Holy Spirit who effects in us our movement into Christ's movement of sacrifice, adoration and communion, who makes us one in Christ, who carries us in him to the Father.

The Spirit and the bride say, 'Come.'
And let everyone who hears say, 'Come.'
And let everyone who is thirsty come.
Let anyone who wishes take the water of life
    as a gift . . .
Amen. Come, Lord Jesus!

(Revelation 22:17, 20b)

TO THE FATHER

The Spirit's prayer in our hearts is 'Abba, Father'. The Spirit is a fountain of living water in us, who says, 'Come to the Father.' Sons in the Son, we are drawn into Christ's irresistible movement of return to the Father, in love. Humankind's ancient nostalgia for the divine, for the Origin, for the One, a nostalgia that is at the root of the religious inspiration of all the great religions, but in a particularly clear way in the Eastern religions, that nostalgia also torments our hearts. But it has a name, the Holy Spirit.

Turned towards the Father, the Spirit in us is desire, prayer of aspiration and expectation, prayer of the pilgrim, prayer of hope. There is an inescapable tension in Christian hope. A theological virtue, its source is in God, it tends towards God in himself, nothing less than God, it is founded on God's promise in Christ. So it is a tension towards the Absolute, infinite audacity.

But hope is also the song of a humble creature walking across space and time towards his homeland, building himself up with the perishable clay of actions which, in themselves, are within the capabilities of historical, contingent human beings. Faith reveals the eternal meaning of these acts accomplished in order to build the world; it does not change their nature. They are our humble and concrete duty.

It is with difficulty that we keep the balance between these two aspects of reality. Either an acute sense of the divine Absolute eclipses that of the humble tasks of earth, and one is in danger of having a disembodied spirituality, which is easily ideological and loses interest in the world and in other people. At the level of the universal Church, that tendency has cost the Church dearly through its passive complicity with terrible individual and social injustices, and the paralysis it has brought about towards the humanist aspirations to assure a life of human dignity for all people. God took on the aspect of enemy of humanity and of life; or, at least, he was the great 'Absent One'.

Or human beings give themselves only too well to their temporal, historical, political or other task. They become intoxicated with their ever-growing power over the created reality that they are building, and consider themselves to be equal to the task in the positive sciences. They altogether lose the sense of the Absolute. They no longer feel the need for God. They wish for and proclaim his death. They want to be their own God, to be their own beginning and end.

We monks, above all we contemplatives, are reproached for being 'disembodied beings', for neglecting our human task,

for being unaware of humankind's true nature, for being para-
sites in the body of humanity. For the atheist it is quite simple.
We are only misfits, defeated people who build for themselves
an imaginary, interior compensation which serves as a cheap
shield from life which is too hard. Even those who believe in
God and in Christ sometimes criticise our flight from the world,
in the name of the Word made flesh who assumed with total
honesty – even to the Cross – the historical reality of human
life. The mark of Christianity, they say, would be precisely the
assumption and transformation of the finite, of the created, by
the divine power.

We must be sufficiently humble to acknowledge that they are
partly right. At times there is flight, ambiguity, in our search
for God in solitude. And Christ really assumed the human and
transformed it. But precisely the human is not confined to
material, social and political tasks, although these tasks have
great importance. But we are beings made for God, with the
capacity for an infinite light and love. In the contemplative,
Christ assumes and transforms in the first place that open heart
of the flesh and blood person: 'Incarnation' of the Word of
God in love. The contemplative's function is to manifest, to
live visibly and institutionally, that dimension of the human
that precisely surpasses humanity (but which is its most essential reality), that ultimate word from the heart to which God
alone, the Absolute and the Infinite, can give a reply.

Thereby, he renders this service to humanity, to remind his
fellow humans where the value of their temporal activity comes
from, and of their end. He tells them that the light of their
intelligence is a reflection of an Eternal Light, to which it
aspires in secret. He assures them that their human love in its
most 'audacious' impulses is right in what it says: Love is
eternal, mutual and total gift. So, let them aspire to it! All
that is beautiful, all wisdom, all communion will have its full
realisation. The contemplative should reveal to his fellow
humans the greatness of their destiny. He should be, at the
heart of humankind, its aspiration towards God. At the heart
of humankind and of creation, and not above them like a pure
spirit. The contemplative's song should be the deepest voice of

the most humble reality: the daily task, the brotherly smile, this yellow flower, this majestic mountain, the sound of a solemn bell, love between friends. All that must be eternal, light, love, and it can be so. It is so, if there is a faith which dares to hope, a love stronger than death, than the nothingness above which the created is suspended. The contemplative's heart is the birth-place of the eternal being of the created. Simplicity – a terrible simplicity is necessary – poverty, transparence and wonder sing, and in singing realise the good news. Christ is born!

The profound movement which has raised up creation since the beginning and throughout all the ages, comes through mys-teriously in symbol, myth, prayer. It takes on a face in Christ and reveals the secret of his eternal youth in the Holy Spirit.

Come, Spirit, come!

33

Waiting for the Spirit (2)

To wait. One awaits what is not there. But we have received the Spirit of Christ. The love of God has been poured into our hearts by the Spirit who is given to us. So, it is not a question of waiting for something that is absent, but of asking that his presence in us may become fully active and efficacious, informing all our faculties and all our acts.

When we call on the Spirit, we do not call on an external reality, but on an interior presence. There is in us, through God's gift, a principle of life, a spring of living water. We are waiting for and asking that this spring may well up and animate our spirit with its light and love. We seek to know God in prayer and contemplation. The source of that knowledge is not primarily outside us, it does not come to us through professors or books, not even through the written word of God (as letter).

These things are necessary, but without the interior light, they are only an unknown language which communicates nothing to us. And the interior light comes from the depth of our heart, where the One who has been given to us in order to lead us to all the truth dwells. Hence the essential importance of the capacity to recollect ourselves deep within us.

Only the human spirit can make known what is truly human. Only the Spirit of God can make God known. The letter is not enough, be it the word of God, be it even the humanity of Christ, the incarnate Word. Only the Spirit vivifies, gives spiritual life in the true sense.

God is not known from without. There is only one knowledge of God, the knowledge he has of himself. All true knowledge of God is a participation in that knowledge, in that pure awareness.

In itself, light does not need light in order to be seen, but, for us, we need objects on which that light can fall and be partly refracted. Thus we need the world in order to see God. What is refracted is precisely what surpasses the object's capacity to absorb; strangely, we reflect what remains a mystery for ourselves.

In contemplation, what counts is not only the object looked at, but the depth with which we look, whether it be at God or the world. What counts is where our gaze is coming from, the light in which we see.

The Spirit is on the side of the subject in the act of contemplation. 'The Lord is my light' (Psalm 27:1). 'In lumine tuo, videbimus lumen' ('In your light we see light') (Psalm 36:9). Not this or that, but light itself. Whether it be a flower, the starry sky or the humanity of Jesus, the most important thing is the quality of the eye's receptivity, of the Spirit who looks through the eye. Its poverty, its availability.

We must become like children to enter the Kingdom of God. Have the limpid, peaceful gaze of a child. 'Happy the poor of heart, the kingdom of heaven is theirs.' To be poor of heart is not to covet what one does not possess, or what one is not. It is to dwell with freedom in the humanity that I am and in the time through which I am passing.

A text from the Statutes brings together these two notions of the Holy Spirit and the depths of the heart. The dweller in cell will be 'led by the Holy Spirit into the depths of his own soul; he is now ready, not only to serve God, but even to cleave to him in love' (Statutes 3.2). That is the work of the Spirit of truth, whom the world cannot receive. There is a kind of interaction between self-knowledge and the knowledge I have of God.

Each one of us, from the same 'objective' revelation, constructs a very subjective image of God. That image is formed partly by my projections, my fears, my desires. The neurotic distorts the truth, the paranoiac projects the internal onto the external, the psychotic denies the external and withdraws into an imaginary world of his own making. According as I integrate my whole reality and no longer need to project parts of it outside myself, according as my gaze does not distort or filter it into external reality, I become more true and capable of more truth. Little by little, I have access to the real and thus I can come closer to him who alone 'is' in the absolute sense. Little by little, I let myself be led by the Spirit of truth.

God is love. The gift of God is the love of God poured into our hearts. Thus, God gives himself to us.

The Spirit is not exactly divine love, which belongs to the divine nature and is possessed by the three Persons in common, let us say. The Spirit is for divine love what the Word is for divine knowledge, its outcome, its fruit. It is difficult to find the word that suits, for 'spirit', in fact, does not come within the compass of *logos*, of the word. In any case, the Spirit's function is that of bond between the Father and the Son, the cohesion of their communion. Let us think of the enormous force that unites the elements of the atom and what happens when it is freed. Pale image.

And the Spirit is given to us, in our hearts. A divine force of love. To us, so weak in love, to us who have such difficulty in not centring the vital force in us on ourselves and in directing it to the other and the Other. We are beings of such fragile identity, so threatened by the instinctual forces from within and the enemy forces from the external world, that we have difficulty in letting go of ourselves in order really to perceive and love the other. So often, our misery binds us.

Our life on earth is a long and laborious gestation in love. Let us never lose courage. God's gift comes to meet our weakness. He first loved us. He gave himself, that is to say, his love, implanted in us, a germ of life that pushes through the opaqueness of our earth with its heaviness and wounds, to break through to the Lord's daylight. In order to enter the Kingdom of God we must be born of water and the Spirit. We must cast off the old skin, be clothed anew in Christ. It is up to us to open ourselves to that vital interior force, to remove the obstacles of our disordered passions, to let ourselves be made in God's image in order to have access, little by little, to gratuitousness, to charity, to love that knows no why, outside itself.

Forgiveness, mercy, gentleness, pity, shared joy, hope, trust, surrender, peace: those are the accents of the Spirit. Let us allow him to speak, to act in us, to realise God's works, God's only work – Christ. Those who are led by the Spirit are children of God, sons in the Son.

One of the works of the Spirit is prayer.

> For all who are led by the Spirit of God are children of God . . . When we cry, 'Abba! Father!' it is that very Spirit bearing witness with our spirit that we are children of God . . . Likewise the Spirit helps us in our weakness; for we do not know how to pray as we ought, but that very Spirit intercedes with sighs too deep for words. And God, who searches the heart, knows what is the mind of the Spirit. (Romans 8:14, 15b–16, 26–27a)

Prayer is not our work. It is the work of the Spirit of the Son. Our whole effort is to pray in the Spirit, as is so often said in the Acts of the Apostles, that is to say, in faith in Christ, in love, in openness to the interior spring, in purity of heart.

At a higher level, it is to let the Spirit pray in us. Our activity boils down to an acquiescence in faith to his prayer in us, a prayer that is little or not at all structured or verbally expressed. It can be silent adoration, a mutual loving look, an indefinable pain which is suffering and desire, joy which expresses itself in a gesture or a song. I am not speaking of a prayer expressing itself through external charisms such as prayer in tongues. That can happen, and that is fine, but that is not the essential. The essential is that the Spirit of God joins our spirit, animates it with that life which he is, life of communion with God, of union between the Son and the Father, of filial movement of love towards the Father. At its most simple – at its best – this prayer is scarcely or not at all distinguishable from life. Thus the Desert tradition spoke of the perfect prayer, which did not know itself to be such.

So this prayer is not something incidental or optional. It is the breathing of our spiritual life, that is, of our life in the Spirit.

It is interesting to note that it was from the phenomenon of our breathing – the breath of our life received, breathed in, then given back, breathed out, and the death that ensues when this breath leaves us – that the people of the Bible first thought of the origin of their life, the Spirit, the *ruah* in Hebrew.

Little by little, the notion was interiorised and differentiated; the human spirit designates the person himself in his most secret intimacy, or in his totality. It distinguishes itself from what is visible, the body, and from what is weak, the flesh.

But the concreteness of the biblical image remains very strong. It is good sometimes to pray to the rhythm of our breathing, as in the prayer of Jesus, or with the prayer, (*breathe in*) 'Come, Holy Spirit, fill our hearts', (*breathe out*) 'kindle in us the fire of your love'. Or simply to feel the movement of life in us in breathing in and out; to receive and to give the fragile substance of our human existence, as light as a feather, and nevertheless, so strong.

The Bible opposes flesh and spirit as two powers that are at work in humankind; the whole person, body and soul, is flesh (*sarx*), in so far as it is sinful and mortal, in so far as it is heaviness, fall towards inertia, congenital weakness. The opposite is the spirit (*pneuma*), a principle of creation, of elevation, of life which advances being towards more life and dynamism, towards its fulfilment, and right into God, who is its essential source. Thus the Spirit is the power and the gift of births and recommencements, of all true creativity, of all spiritual pursuit.

Humankind left to its nature alone has difficulty in entering into God's plans. The Lord's thoughts are not our thoughts. We always have to be converted, to struggle against the heaviness of the flesh, to broaden the spaces of our spirit, to have access in the obscurity of faith, at times in anguish, but also in trust, to the thinking of God and his love concerning us.

On the other hand, what the Spirit is capable of is revealed in Christ, above all in the Risen Christ, in whom the fullness of life unfolds without obstacle. And since we are animated by the same Spirit, we also hope to enter the world of the Resurrection. Meanwhile, on earth, to be animated by the Spirit of God is to walk in the footsteps of Christ, to have the same sentiments, the same love for others, the same mercy, the same solidarity, the same forgiveness, the same humility and the same gentleness.

It is to have one's eyes always fixed on the Father, to let the Father do his works and speak his words in us. It is always to do the Father's will. It is to suffer (if he wishes and for his glory) contradiction, rejection, suffering, in peace and without bitterness.

It is to have an unlimited trust in the Father's love and in his providence. It is to have no anxiety about ourselves, but to surrender ourselves in total simplicity, for death and for life, to him who is eternal Life and Love.

Maranatha! Come, Lord Jesus!

34

Waiting for the Spirit (3)

This is for those who would like to be and to pray together while waiting for the Spirit, in a general way or with a view to some special grace or healing. (Therefore, those who prefer can remain in cell or attend only part of it.)

No recreation this Sunday.

After None, go to the Novitiate conference room.

Take up the position you prefer (seated, standing etc.).

Remain in silence for a time long enough to have allowed the inclinations to say or do something immediately to pass. Go within yourself, be together.

Then, let this communion express itself, if it wishes, in a gesture, a word, or again by silence. Someone may feel the need for a precise healing for which he will request the prayer of all, or another may want to be reconciled with God or with a brother, and so on. Each one is free to follow the Spirit in him; no one is obliged to do anything whatsoever.

All these were constantly devoting themselves to prayer [in the Upper Room where they were], together with ... Mary, the mother of Jesus, as well as his brothers. (Acts 1:14)

PENTECOST

35

The Coming of the Holy Spirit

**'I came to bring fire to the earth,
and how I wish it were already kindled!'**

(Luke 12:49)

The spectacular descent of the Holy Spirit ends the celebration of Easter. The inspired dream of the prophets comes true. The power of the Paschal mystery takes possession of the disciples and transforms them.

The Spirit descends on each Christian at the moment of his Baptism; he is given with all his gifts. That presence becomes more intense, more efficacious, every time we open ourselves to it through a more living faith, a stronger hope, a more ardent love. It is to that that the Liturgy invites and urges us; at this time, it has a special power to realise it. So we are going to meditate on this mystery by opening wide our heart so that it may permeate us, at this very moment, with its power.

THE FIRST PENTECOST

A small group of men, of very humble circumstances, is together in a room in Jerusalem. It has been their custom for some weeks, since their leader was crucified. The city police have indeed noticed this gathering; they leave them alone. This handful of men is not dangerous. They have not the makings of revolutionaries. At the death of the Nazarene, they fled like cowards. From the provinces, ignorant and stubborn, a little het up, that's all. Men speak of a reappearance of Jesus, of a so-called resurrection! Women's tale, no doubt. The great city crucified Christ. He is dead. Now she calmly forgets him. The matter is shelved.

What exactly happened on the first Pentecost? Everything, in this upper room where Jesus celebrated the first Eucharist, evokes his presence, the sound of his voice, the promises of the Paraclete whom he was going to send upon them, 'power from on high' (Luke 24:49). Mary, his mother, is there. Around her forms a home of prayer, of faith, of hope. Their eyes are turned towards heaven. They wait. The Spirit comes: sudden and abrupt irruption, sound of a violent gust of wind that fills the house. Then, tongues of fire appear; they divide and come to rest on each one of the disciples. That fire seems to permeate them, effecting an intimate metamorphosis. All of them, filled with the Holy Spirit, begin 'to speak in other languages, as the Spirit gave them ability'. Filled with a holy elation, their voices rise in ecstatic transports of praise. The strange thing, the people from all countries who flocked to them, heard them, each one in his own language. Oneness of human language, broken at the Tower of Babel because of human pride (Genesis 11:1–9), is re-established through the gift of the Spirit. The Spirit is able to make himself understood by people of all languages. Love is one, its language is discerned deep down in the human heart.

The Spirit who hovered over the primeval waters, the creative breath of God, rests on the disciples, forms them into a new creation. They are transformed into intrepid witnesses, these poor Galileans who up to now remained in hiding for fear of danger. Peter boldly addresses the crowd, refutes their cunning remarks, outlines the mystery of Christ with vigorous strokes, is not afraid to remind them of their guilt. 'Let the entire house of Israel know with certainty that God has made him both Lord and Messiah, this Jesus whom you crucified' (Acts 2:36).

With hearts deeply moved, they hear those fiery words. 'What will we do, brothers?' Peter thunders: 'Repent, and be baptized every one of you in the name of Jesus Christ so that your sins may be forgiven; and you will receive the gift of the Holy Spirit' (Acts 2:38).

The conversions are not long in coming, three thousand on the first day. Thus is born the first community, first stage of the Church's prodigious expansion which the Spirit is going

to bring about thanks to the preaching of the Apostles. The fire
is cast on the earth. The enthusiasm it kindles is not something
superficial and transient. It is lasting. It finds expression in an
effective action and an heroic witness; many of these inspired
ones are going to seal it with their blood. It is the intoxication
of the Spirit promised by the prophets for the last times, when
God will come to establish his Kingdom in a definitive way
among humankind. With the Resurrection of Christ and the
outpouring of the Spirit, that time is inaugurated. The
Kingdom of God is among us, is in us. Peter does not hesitate to
apply the famous prophecy of Joel to the miracle of Pentecost.

> In the last days it will be, God declares,
>   that I will pour out my Spirit upon all flesh,
>   and your sons and your daughters shall prophesy,
>   and your young men shall see visions,
>   and your old men shall dream dreams.
>
> (Acts 2:17=Joel 3:1–2)

All the Acts of the Apostles, the Gospel of the Spirit, recounts
the fulfilment of that prophecy.

THE ACTUALITY OF PENTECOST

This account recovers all its actuality in the light of the recent
proliferation of outpourings of the Spirit in a way that is remi-
niscent of the first Pentecost, above all by the gift of speaking
in tongues – glossolalia. Commentators and theologians have,
in general, succeeded for a long time in fossilising the extraordinary events of the first Pentecost, like venerated objects of
an antique dealer. It was a question of an initial impetus given
to the missionary expansion of the Church, become
unnecessary for a Church equipped with a solid structure and
a developed doctrinal expression. For us, the hierarchy and a
dogmatic faith should be enough. One was not going to bother
the Spirit by asking him to effect something extraordinary. One
left that to the peripheral groups who insisted on reading Sacred
Scripture in a fundamentalist manner, that is to say, literally.

There is wisdom in this view, but a wisdom, perhaps, that is too human. In practice, one runs the risk of reducing the Church to the level of a human institution, faith to something too reasonable, the Christian life to a rather dull attainment of middle-class respectability which is far too prudent and proper. The Spirit has taken upon himself to shatter those reasonings in an explosion of gifts, among people who have taken seriously the reality of the gift of the Spirit that they received at Baptism and who earnestly asked the Spirit to come and revive his gifts by the breath of his power. The Spirit has responded, and Pentecost recurs in our days.

Maybe the Church's present situation is returning to conditions that are (and will be more so) analogous to those of the first days: small minority communities, dispersed in a neutral or hostile mass. In any case, the Spirit is operating, that is certain. Each of us should become aware that he must be open to accept the movement of the Spirit whom he received with sanctifying grace. We possess all the gifts of the Spirit. Let us open ourselves in all simplicity to the power of the Spirit, with a truly living faith, so that the Spirit may act in us, that in him and by him alone, we may live, love and pray at the level of our Christian being.

GLOSSOLALIA

One of the most disconcerting manifestations of the Spirit's action is the 'speaking in tongues'. What exactly is it about? First of all, one must distinguish between 'speaking' in an unknown language and the ecstatic prayer that finds expression in inarticulate sounds. The first seems to come within the category of the miracle. The first Pentecost is an example of that. It comes to pass very rarely.

The second does not seem to be miraculous in itself. It is not, in principle, pathological either. It cannot be reduced to a phenomenon of collective emotion or hysteria, or of infantilism. Competent psychologists are in agreement on this point, although one has to admit that there are probably pathological elements in a certain number of cases. (That is accidental and does not belong to the essence of the charism.)

So how do we understand glossolalia, and what is its meaning? The phenomenon is acknowledged to be real in Sacred Scripture: in the Acts (2:4–11; 10:46; 19:6), in St Paul (1 Corinthians 12:30; 13:1; 14:2, 39) and in Mark's Gospel (16:17), in which Jesus promises his own they will speak in tongues. St Paul will say that this gift is the most modest of all, that he himself possesses it and wishes it for others, but that one must see to it that there is order and decorum when it is exercised in public assemblies. So, one cannot deny that it has a biblical basis. Besides, it is to be found across the lived tradition of the Church: at the beginning in a rather widespread way, then more rarely, except in the lives of the saints. So it must be taken seriously.

If one examines this gift from the phenomenological point of view, it appears as a verbal expression whose organisation is not ordered by a linguistic structure. Other examples: the 'jubilation' of the Alleluia in an Easter Mass; or the sounds through which a little child shows his joy. Prayer in tongues, it has been said, is to ordinary prayer what abstract art is to representational painting.

Glossolalia is not diminished by situating it on a natural level. It is just like the gift of tears. To shed tears is something natural. But at times, by a gift of the Spirit, it can become the expression of a deep and ineffable religious experience. In this case, the meaning of the tears transcends their materiality. Likewise, 'speaking in tongues', though natural in itself, can sometimes be the expression of the working of the Holy Spirit.

Its religious value

What is its religious value? Trustworthy testimonies of reliable people testify that 'this mode of prayer is a form of release from oneself, of freeing, of interior liberation before God and others'. It is 'a mode of prayer beyond words and beyond all cerebralism. It gives rise to peace and a blossoming of life.'* People who have experienced it remark that it seems to effect a breach

---

* *A New Pentecost?* (Cardinal Suenens).

in their habitual system of reserve and defence through a kind
of self-surrender to the Lord, that permits the Spirit to deploy
his action and his other gifts in them. Considering that it is
only a kind of initial trigger, it is none the less precious for
that.

In psychological language one would say that it is the voice
of the subconscious that rises up towards God. It is an
expression of our subconscious just as dreams, laughter, tears,
painting and dance are. It is acted out in the depths of our
being: hence the result of deep healing that is often attributed
to it, healing of hidden traumatisms that prevent the blossoming
of the interior life.

Let us admit that we are, in general, terribly complex when
it is a question of expressing our deep religious sentiments as
much with God as with others. We have been steeped in formalism and ritualism. We have difficulty in finding the warmth
suitable for a feast, for a fraternal encounter. We need to renew
contact with body-language, no less than with the non-
conceptual depths of our being.

St Paul assures us that 'that very Spirit intercedes with sighs
too deep for words' (Romans 8:26b). It is to this mysterious
inarticulate prayer that glossolalia unites us, leaving to the Spirit
himself the task of glorifying God and thanking him for a love
'that surpasses knowledge' (Ephesians 3:19).

'Speaking in tongues', thus understood, seems like a spiritual
enrichment and a fruit of grace.

The essential is the unhindered openness of our whole being
to God's action, to the prayer of the Spirit in us. In the framework of our life, the manifestations of that openness will
normally be more discreet. The Spirit's action in the life of the
solitary, in general, and in prayer in particular, is often quite
hidden. Everything happens at a deep level. Love has its
modesty.

For all that, I do not wish you exactly the gift of glossolalia.
But I do wish that you may open all the doors of your being to
the Spirit's action, including your sensibility and your unconscious; that you may allow the deep waves of the ineffable

prayer of the Spirit to flow in your expanded hearts; that our community life and choral prayer may allow something of the freedom, spontaneity and warmth of the Spirit to show through.

> Living fountain, fire, love,
> anointing that permeates souls.
> Open our senses to your light,
> pour into our hearts your love.

THE GIFT OF THE SPIRIT

The Gospel of Pentecost Sunday is new: instead of reading, as was formerly the case, one of the promises of the sending of the Spirit (John 14:23–31), we again take the first part of the Gospel of the second Sunday of Easter. Thus is realised a very Johannine inclusion of that series of Gospels from the second to the seventh Sunday of Easter. The unity of the different aspects of the Paschal mystery is strongly insisted upon, for St John shows us Jesus in person, on the very evening of the Resurrection, having recalled his relationship with the Father, sending the Spirit on the disciples, and thus enabling them to continue his mission of redemption in the world.

> 'As the Father has sent me, so I send you.' When he had said this, he breathed on them and said to them, 'Receive the Holy Spirit. If you forgive the sins of any, they are forgiven them; if you retain the sins of any, they are retained.' (John 20:21–23)

The gift of the Spirit gives humankind a specifically divine power, for only God can forgive sins. The Spirit's presence is a presence of mercy, forgiveness and healing; a presence visible in the Church and the sacrament of forgiveness. Thus Christ touches and heals people of every age to the end of the world.

It is lovely to finish our meditation of Eastertide on this note of God's merciful love. That is why John 3:16–21 has been retained as the Gospel of the Monday* after Pentecost. It is like an echo that still rings in the air when the celebration, strictly speaking, of the Fifty Days is over; an echo, aroused by the heart itself, of the greatest of the mysteries.

> 'For God so loved the world that he gave his only Son, so that everyone who believes in him may not perish but may have eternal life.' (John 3:16)

May this force of love not remain in the sanctuary. May it inform our whole life.

> I therefore, the prisoner in the Lord, beg you to lead a life worthy of the calling to which you have been called, with all humility and gentleness. (Ephesians 4:1–2, Scripture reading of the Monday after Pentecost)

. . . with all love.

Come, Lord Jesus!

---

* We know that in strict liturgy the celebration of Easter should finish on Pentecost Sunday. The prolongation to the Monday is the result of the following circumstance: we remain in solitude for the big feasts, and the time spent together that ought to mark them is deferred to the following day. Perhaps it would be better to regard it as a sort of echo rather than as a prolongation.